The book is dedicated to Abram Leon, Jew and revolutionary, who was
murdered in Auschwitz at the age of 26.

**Cover illustration: Christine Gray**

**Acknowledgements for photographs**
2-5, Rollins Collection at Modern Records Centre,
Warwick University.
7, Manchester Studies Unit, Manchester
Polytechnic (special thanks to Don)

ISBN 0 9509636 0 7

Published by:
*Beyond the Pale Collective*
*Box No 6,*
*59, Cookridge Street,*
*Leeds,*
*LS2 3AW*
*ENGLAND*

Typeset, designed and printed by:
Manchester Free Press,
Bombay House,
59 Whitworth Street,
Manchester
M1 3WT

Distributors:
Scottish and Northern Book Distribution
48a Hamilton Place
Edinburgh
EH3 5AX (Scottish Office)
031-225 4950

4th Floor
18 Granby Row
Manchester
M1 3GE (Northern Office)
061-228 3903

Turnaround Distribution
27, Horsell Road,
London N5
01-609 7836

# That's Funny You Don't Look Anti-Semitic

## An anti-racist analysis of left anti-semitism

by Steve Cohen
Edited and produced by Libby Lawson
and Erica Burman.

# Contents

# Why is this book different from all other books?

In all other books we are not allowed to see anti-semitism, let alone the anti-semitism of the Left.
*But in this book we can.*

In all other (non-feminist) books we do not identify the links between Jews, Blacks and women.
*But in this book we do.*

In all other books we are told to assimilate or go to Israel.
*But in this book we need not do either.*

In all other books we can be either Jewish or Left.
*But in this book we can be both.*

---

Beyond the Pale Collective comprises:
Erica Burman and Libby Lawson.

We would like to thank the Collective for being there when we needed them, for endless cups of tea, for providing help and encouragement when the going got rough while editing, producing and publishing this book. They made it all possible!

Beyond the Pale Collective

# Introduction

This book is written from a perspective of communism and anti-racism. It is, naturally, opposed to anti-semitism in whatever guise. In particular, it is a polemic against manifestations of anti-semitism by those who claim to be part of the socialist or communist tradition. It has been a painful piece to write, intellectually and emotionally. I guess it will be painful to read. Leon Trotsky once said that **"only the truth is revolutionary"**. This was his answer to those who refused to criticise Stalinism for fear that imperialists would jump on these criticisms, to further attack the very real achievements of the Bolshevik revolution. The facts in the book might well provide some perverse ammunition to reactionaries of all kinds, who want to denounce revolutionary change. So be it. Reaction has to be defeated honestly, not by defending the indefensible; what is written here is not in any way presented as a last word, rather it is an attempt to open up a genuine debate on the Left. Hopefully, something positive will emerge from the dissection of such negative material.

Even in draft form, the book has been attacked by individuals on the Left and the Right. However, what has made it possible and worthwhile has been the tremendous encouragement from so many different people (many of whom I have never met). Not least are those who have donated the entire cost of the production. I would like to thank Manchester Jewish Socialist Group for their support—in particular Joe Garman and Jeremy Green for their midnight discussion. I would also like to thank all those women in the women's caucus at the national Jewish Socialist Group day school on Left Anti-semitism, who forcefully expressed their desire for publication. Francesca Klug and Judy Keiner wrote me extremely long and constructive letters, helping to clarify many points and raising further ones. Bill Williams spent years, literally, discussing the issues raised in the book. Finally, limitless thanks to Libby Lawson and Erica Burman who kidnapped the manuscript after it had been through countless drafts and, by editing it, made sure that it is Kosher and fit for human consumption.

All money that is received through sales will go to *Shifra* magazine, which is about to be produced by a Jewish feminist collective. So buy!

# The Socialism of Fools

To struggle as a Jewish socialist it is a distinct advantage to have been born with three hands—at least three hands. On the one hand it is necessary to struggle against the anti-semitism of daily life both in its casual and its organised forms. On the other hand, it is necessary to struggle against the reactionary Jewish communal leadership which simultaneously advocates zionism in Israel and a form of assimilation in the diaspora as the fulfilment of Jewish identity. On the third hand, it is necessary to resist the anti-semitism that has permeated much of the socialist tradition and which was described by August Bebel, German Social Democrat leader, as the **"socialism of fools"**.

This book is about Left anti-semitism and is written as a contribution to the anti-racist struggle. Contemporary socialist practice is self-critical enough, albeit to a limited and inadequate extent, to acknowledge that an examination of its own anti-black racism is a legitimate exercise. At the very least, socialists will be prepared to admit that national chauvinism may be present in their own groups. Whatever commitment there is to this, self-criticism has only come about through the existence and pressure of autonomous black organisations and black resistance. However, any attempt to raise even a discussion about the anti-semitic nature of much socialist practice is almost invariably met with apoplexy and vilification. It is virtually a taboo subject.

The reasons why it is essential to study Left anti-semitism are self-evident. Firstly, just as we look to reject the reactionary elements within the Jewish heritage and seek to build only on what is positive, so likewise we have to disregard all reactionary elements that have

9

entered socialism. This is particularly the case with socialism, as it is a movement aimed at changing the entire world and claims to be based on theories of consciousness: hence lack of consciousness of anti-semitism within socialist practice opens up major questions about that practice. Secondly, the Left has often found itself complicit in anti-semitism, and this has had a profound effect on Jewish identity: it has driven many Jews away from socialism, despite the fact that Jewish people played an important role in the development of the socialist movement from its inception. The Jewish masses were active from the Bund (the revolutionary union of Jewish workers) of Russia and Poland to the major movements of Jewish anarchists and communists in this country. These movements were also of significance within the Jewish community itself and were often able to challenge the Jewish establishment. Today this has all but disappeared. Socialists who have an awareness of their Jewishness are isolated inside the Left and have almost no base within the Jewish community.

There are many reasons for this—not least the triumphant anti-communism of the communal leadership. However, one other particular reason is that socialism has appeared to offer no answers to Jewish people and has been seen as tainted with anti-semitism. This is highly significant within the Stalinist tradition because of the generations of Jews who joined or identified with the Communist Parties of the Third International, only to be disillusioned. The socialism of fools, though, also appears both with the reformism of social democracy and with the revolutionary groupings that have dissociated themselves from both reformism and Stalinism. It is not surprising therefore, that so many Jews have turned away from socialism.

## Anti-Semitism

It is not difficult to construct a catalogue of grotesque statements and actions by socialists with respect to Jewish people. These are bad enough in themselves and should be opposed from any anti-racist perspective. However, the purpose of this book is to show that Left anti-semitism cannot be understood empirically, merely as a series of unrelated descriptions or examples: rather there is a pattern, a methodology, of Left anti-semitism.

This methodology is by no means confined to the Left. It exists in society at large. It provides anti-semitism with its uniqueness as a form of racism and hence with its definition as a specific category.

Anti-semitism is not simply a type of national chauvinism that happens to be directed against Jews—although this is obviously an important aspect of it. Though Jewish people have suffered and are suffering horrifically from the material consequences of anti-semitism, its uniqueness cannot be located merely in this material suffering. The peculiar and defining feature of anti-semitism is that it exists as an **ideology.** It provides its adherents with a universal and generalised interpretation of the world. This is the theory of the Jewish conspiracy, which depicts Jews as historically controlling and determining nature and human destiny. Anti-semitism is an ideology which has influenced millions of people precisely because it presents an explanation of the world by attributing such extreme powers to its motive force—the Jews. For instance, Arnold White, a fanatical advocate of Jewish immigration control into the U.K. at the turn of the century, wrote that

> **"Jewish power... baffled the Pharoahs, foiled Nebuchadnessar, thwarted Rome, defeated feudalism, circumvented the Romanovs, balked the Kaiser and undermined the Third French Republic."**
> *(The Modern Jew)*

The ancient roots of anti-semitism as ideology can perhaps be found in the pre-Christian world. From the time of the Babylonian exile in the 6th century B.C., most Jews lived outside Palestine and were subjected to accusations of disloyalty because of their allegiance to a god which was not only monotheistic and therefore omnipotent, but which was also supra-national. Jews had a loyalty beyond that to the particular kingdom in which they resided. However, the development of anti-semitism as a **theory** is a consequence of Christianity.

Christianity transformed notions of Jewish disloyalty into a fundamentally demonic view of the entire world: it equated Jewry with a universal satanic influence. Such an equation is probably inherent within Christianity, as a theology, because of the identification of Jews with the crucifixion. As the Gospel of St. John says of Jews:

> **"You are of your father the devil and your will is to do your father's desires. He was a murderer from the beginning."**

The Christian church was promulgating such a theory as early as the 2nd. century, whilst engaging in a highly political struggle with the synagogue for converts in the Hellenistic world and when, indeed, each was still struggling to win adherents from the other. As Norman

11

Cohn has written in *Warrant For Genocide*:

> "It was to terrorise the judaising Christians of Antioch into a final breach with the parent religion that St. John Chrysostom called the synagogue 'the temple of demons... the cavern of devils... a gulf and an abyss of perdition' and portrayed Jews as habitual murderers and destroyers, people possessed by an evil spirit. And it was to protect his catechumens against Judaism that St. Augustine described those who had been the favourite sons of God as now transformed into sons of Satan. Moreover the Jews were brought into relation with that fearsome figure Antichrist 'the son of perdition' whose tyrannical reign, according to St. Paul and the Book of Revelations, is to precede the second coming of Christ. Many of the fathers taught that Antichrist would be a Jew and that the Jews would be his most devoted followers."

This mythology flowered with a vengeance and gained popular acceptance during the Catholic church's most militant period—the crusades. Here Jews were presented as the Devil's offspring—ritually murdering Christian children, poisoning the wells and torturing the consecrated wafer. Apart from anything else, this led to murderous attacks on many Jewish communities in Europe. For instance, the Third Crusade (1189-92) commanded wide support in England where it led to attacks by the assembled crusaders on Jews in various towns, especially York. It would be patently inadequate to regard the crusades simply as a war with Islam. They also represent the final victory and consolidation of Christian hegemony within Europe itself. This was the period when Christianity finally began routing paganism—both physically and by expropriating myths. On one hand, pagan festivals were incorporated into Christian holy days, on the other hand, popular folk perceptions of the evil eye were synthesised into anti-semitism.

It is possible to develop a materialist and class analysis of anti-semitism which relates the ideology of Jewish domination to underlying economic and social changes. The most obvious example of this is the way the conspiracy theory became secularised in the 18th. and 19th. centuries. It was at the end of the 19th. century that the mass circulation of the *Protocols of the Learned Elders of Zion* began. This document purported to show that there actually existed a Jewish government which met in secret and which exercised international political power through its control of the media and of the banks. It metamorphosised the devil into a world parliament of Jews. This secularisation was, in reality, nothing more than a reflection of the secularisation of social life as a whole—not least as manifested through the development of the national secular state.

However, a crude deterministic analysis is out of place here. The form of anti-semitism as ideology may change but its essence remains intact, independant of the economic formation under which it is operating. Indeed, the supposed secularisation of the conspiracy theory in the age of rationalism was inevitably flimsy—as the theory itself is profoundly irrational: it grew out of demonology and it always returns to demonology. Ultimately, anti-semitism is about the cosmos and not simply a world parliament. This demonology surfaced in its most powerful way in the middle of the 20th. century with the rise of Nazism. Nazism had no pretence that anti-semitism was anything other than devil-power. As Hitler is quoted as saying:

**"It is the inexorable Jew who struggles for his domination...  Two worlds face one another, the men of God and the men of Satan. The Jew is the anti-man, the creature of another God... I set the Aryan and the Jew ever and against each other"** (Davidowicz—*The War Against the Jews*).

Anti-semitism is a classic example of how not simply pre-capitalist, but also pre-feudal formulations, can flourish in capitalist (and in the case of the U.S.S.R.) post-capitalist societies.

As an ideology anti-semitism is irrationalism par excellence. Moreover, its proponents do not deny this irrationalism—they exalt it. Since anti-semitism takes as given that Jew-power determines history, then the fact that it determines it in seemingly contradictory ways is simply part of the conspiracy. Hence Jews can apparently be dominating the world simultaneously through capitalism and through communism; through sexually corrupting non-Jews and through keeping themselves isolated sexually by not intermarrying; through being cosmopolitans without a nation state and through being zionists. Literally everything can fit into the conspiracy. It is infinite. Even Nazism can, since its defeat, be seen as part of the conspiracy. The Australian fascist Eric Butler in his book *The International Jew, The Truth about the Protocols of Zion*, claims that Hitler was himself a tool of the conspiracy and was seeking to further the international dispersal of Jews. One of the fearsome features of anti-semitism is that while its essence remains the same its shape is constantly shifting and enlarging as it accumulates more myths. This increase can either be gradual or explosive, depending on the social and political situation. Its nearest equivalent in the realm of natural phonomena, is that of the ever-expanding universe where the constant energy source of the initial big bang is represented in Christian culture by the ceaseless responsibility given to Jews for the crucifixion.

## Anti-Semitism without Jews

The ultimate 'full-circle' irrationalism of anti-semitism as an ideology is that it does not actually need Jews. There can be anti-semitism without a single Jew. This is precisely because anti-semitism is an ideology which claims to provide cosmic understanding. Central to the ideology are demonic notions which quite clearly transcend the material presence of Jews. Many examples can be given of this. Thus the identification of Jewry with the devil makes Jewry responsible for all satanic influences, including humanity's original sin—the Fall in Eden—which, even according to Judeo-Christian mythology, took place before the identifiable existence of Jews.

Again, if the almost unimaginable had occurred and the holocaust had been successful in its declared aim, then it would be ludicrous to think this would have been the end to anti-semitism. If anything, it would have been its historical triumph. The ideology would have remained, and if Nazism would ever have felt the need for a material presence of Jews it would simply have designated particular individuals as Jews. Indeed, Nazi law did invent its own definition of Jewry which did not necessarily relate to Jews' self-definition. Apparently in the Warwaw ghetto there was a Catholic church which opened for practising Catholics, who were designated as Jews by the Nazis, and who were destroyed in the same gas chambers as Jews (see David Ruben, 'Marxism and the Jewish Question', *Socialist Register* 1982). Similarly, in Poland today anti-semitism, under the guise of anti-zionism, exists even though the bulk of the Jewish population has been destroyed. Anti-semitism is apparently unique in that not only does it perceive its victim, the Jew, as having ultimate power, but this perception also remains even when there are no victims left alive.

Perhaps the ideologies of all class societies are based on a completely negative form of irrationalism—because such societies combine both irrationalism and negativity. Maybe if all other assumptions were swept away, then sexism and anti-black racism would also be exposed as resting on the fear by men, or white people,

14

that women or black people had ultimate control. However, sexism and anti-black racism are different phenomena which operate in different ways from each other, and both operate differently from anti-semitism.

The distinguishing feature of anti-semitism is that for its ideologues the conspiracy theory operates on the surface—it is visible. No other assumption has to be pulled away for it to be revealed—it **is** the assumption. For instance, according to National Front mythology, even the very presence of black people in the U.K. is part of a Jewish conspiracy.

It is of course true that there have been historical periods where sexism has operated as an almost explicit conspiracy theory. For example, in medieval times, witches and homosexuals, men and women, formed, along with Jews, the unholy trinity of the Antichrist. In particular, images of Jews and of witches as sorcerers and defilers, were often interchangeable. Again, beneath the surface of much anti-black racism lurks fear of voodoo and occult rituals.

What gives sexism and racism their own unique irrationalism, however, is precisely the fact that notions of conspiracy are rarely explicit. They are normally quite hidden and therefore in this way harder to combat. It is not coincidental, nor any more reassuring, that there is not a plethora of explicit literature on a supposed world conspiracy of women, gays or black people. Indeed medieval witch massacres had to make a profoundly nonsensical distinction between witches and "good" women. There is no hierarchy of oppression— but each operates in its own frightening way.

There is no reason to assume that individual anti-semites have an explicit world conspiracy theory—just as there is no reason to assume, for example, that capitalist traders have a fully worked-out theoretical appreciation of bourgeois economics. Many Jew-haters just seize on particular anti-semitic images of Jews—as bloodsuckers, usurers or whatever. These images have been within Christendom and accumulating, one on another, for nearly two millenia. In terms of individual psychology, false consciousness of the conspiracy theory is usually quite fragmented—individuals will carry around some anti-Jewish images in an ad hoc manner.

The distinguishing feature of anti-semitism is the success and persistence of the attempts which its most powerful ideologues, from the early Christian fathers, to the crusaders, to the Protocols, to the Nazi philosophers, have made to theorise it in terms of the conspiracy of Jews. The anti-semitism of daily life, whether or not it is understood by its adherents, all takes place within this theoretical framework. Moreover, popular consciousness about Jews, however individually fragmented, is sufficiently potent to be regularly stimulated by demagogues into a mass psychology—by demagogues who have genuine awareness of conspiracy theory. Fascist politicians in this century have well understood this.

## Left Anti-Semitism

Anti-semitism on the Left is essentially identical to, and has the same methodology as, that of society at large. It is the expession of the conspiracy theory—but under the false guise of socialism. Usurping the language of class struggle it negates the very idea of class struggle and replaces it with anti-Jewish struggle.

Of course, socialist practice is not a monolith. Some of it has accorded with socialist theory and has **not** been anti-semitic. Inasmuch as that has any relevance to the present debate, however, it is relevant only to the **weight** of the anti-semitic tradition within socialist practice. It neither explains nor denies that tradition. Moreover, there is no balance sheet with any form of racism. It is hardly worthwhile to subtract the number of racist statements made from the number of non-racist statements to calculate how racist a movement is. Why bother? It is intolerable that socialist practice should contain any anti-semitism and it is equally intolerable that a wall of silence, often to the point of censorship, should have been thrown around its existence. Indeed, there is some hypocrisy present here. Many socialists, and many socialist organisations, will wish to distance themselves from any insinuations about their own anti-semitic practice, precisely by claiming that the Left tradition has not been monolithic. However, if it has not been so monolithic in their eyes, then it is perfectly legitimate to ask why they have consistently remained silent and complicit in the face of Left anti-semitism.

This book is primarily about socialist practice in the U.K. in general, and England in particular. However, this practice also comes out of a European tradition of socialism, so inevitably, references are made to other movements outside the U.K.—including those in the U.S.S.R. and the U.S.A. The book says nothing about socialist or liberation movements in the third world, deliberately so, because countries in the third world have not historically been within the grip of Christianity, and thus have no tradition of conspiracy theories. For instance, within Islam both Jew and Christian were seen as infidels—and certainly there was no constant mythology of universal Jewish domination. If notions about Jewish power have entered the third world, then that is a product of imperialistic and Christian penetration.

Left anti-semitism has gone through two distinct, if related and overlapping, stages. The first coincided with the establishment of the modern socialist movement itself, at the end of the 19th. century. Here, the particular mythology of Jew as finance capitalist took root within important sectors of the emergent socialist and industrial labour movement. This was crucial, as it meant that socialist practice had a tradition of anti-semitism almost from its birth. The second stage developed around the question of zionism—particularly after the war which created Israel in 1948. A significant feature of contemporary socialist practice is, on the one hand, the expansion of zionism to equate it with world imperialist domination and, on the other hand, the reduction of the entire Jewish experience to equate **that** with zionism. It is a combination of the conspiracy theory with that of collective guilt.

Quite clearly, anti-zionism is not in itself anti-semitic. However, much of what the Left poses as anti-zionism is transcendental: it relates neither to the struggle of the Palestinians nor to what the Israeli state is actually doing. Rather it is concerned with ascribing world power to zionism and holding all Jews in the world responsible for this. Left practice presents as anti-zionism something which is neither about zionism nor about Palestinian liberation, but is about some alleged responsibility of Jews on a global scale. This is anti-semitism.

The fact that this book is written in full support of the Palestinian struggle is absolutely irrelevant. Left anti-semitism has to be condemned irrespective of one's position on zionism. However, socialist Jews who are committed equally to solidarity with the Palestinian liberation struggle and to the fight against anti-semitism, are put in an impossible "catch 22" situation by the Left. Any mention of anti-semitism is seen as a diversion from the struggle against zionism. Moreover, the merest suggestion that the Left can itself be anti-semitic is equated with an attack, both on communism, and on the Palestinian cause. An example, which is almost a caricature, occurred in an editorial in the journal *Big Flame* which stated that an "obsession" with anti-semitism detracted from the need to "focus" on zionism (October, 1982).

There is, manifestly, an ideological link between the anti-semitism present at the birth of a definitive socialist practice in the last century, and Left anti-semitism in relation to zionism in this century. It would be anti-dialectical to expect the disappearance of ideological deformations without their being consciously challenged. There is also a specific ideological linkage uniting the two historical periods and running like a chain between them. This is assimilationism. The general chauvinism which permeates the Left on matters of cultural and national identity has assumed such a form that an independent Jewish identity is seen as either conceptually impossible or hopelessly reactionary. The relationship between assimilationism and anti-semitism as ideology is a problematic one, and is looked at later. What is being emphasised here is the strength of assimilationism within socialist thought.

## Socialism, Anti-Semitism, Thatcherism and Fascism

Anti-semitism on the Left is harmful to Jews and degrading to socialists, irrespective of the precise historical period in which it manifests itself. However, there is a particular urgency in facing up to it today. We are now witnessing a popular resurgence of the New Right, best exemplified by Thatcherism in the U.K. As well as being a direct attack on the working class this represents chauvinism in all aspects—racial national and sexual. It is arguable whether anti-semitism could become an explicit part of Tory philosophy. It certainly has popular appeal and is an important component of the "Victorian Values" that this government is so fond of espousing. However, it may well be that even the Tory Party could not incorporate anti-semitism institutionally in the direct way that all parliamentary parties now incorporate anti-black racism. Arguably, this requires a party of open fascism.

In any event, it is inconceivable that a socialist movement which is shot through with its own anti-semitism could face up to any of the aspects of Tory, let alone fascist, chauvinism. Over the last few years, sections of the socialist movement, mainly stimulated by the ideas and attitudes of feminism, have been re-evaluating their practice in order to develop a socialist practice which is both aware of the aspirations of the oppressed and is unoppressive in itself. This book about Left anti-semitism is written in that spirit.

# The Anti-Semitism of English Socialism's Formative Years

## The Background

The period 1880 to 1914 is central to understanding how anti-semitism has permeated much of the socialist tradition. This was an epoch which witnessed:

(a) the consolidation of world imperialism

(b) the formation of the first self-styled socialist organisations such as the Social Democratic Federation—the S.D.F.—and the Independent Labour Party—the I.L.P.

(c) the development of industrial trades unionism.

The impact of imperialism was to imbue the labour movement and the socialist organisation with national and chauvinistic ideas—ideas which persist today. Another phenomenon also occurred in these years—the mass immigration of Jews into England as they fled from the progroms of Russia and Eastern Europe.

The immigrants arrived into a country that was already deeply anti-semitic. Anti-semitism in England had existed well before imperialism or capitalism. It was pre-feudal and rooted in Christianity. The entire Jewish population had already been forcibly expelled by Edward 1st. in 1290. Readmitted by Cromwell, they were ghettoised and portrayed through popular mythology as Shylocks and Fagins. It is not surprising, therefore, that Jews in the 1880's were greeted by anti-semitism on arrival. A significant consequence of this was that the chauvinism of the socialist and labour movement became fuelled by a specific and virulent anti-semitism. Like all anti-semitism this was based, to a greater or lesser extent, on notions of the world Jewish conspiracy.

The most obvious example of this was the equation of Jews with capitalism—the classic socialism of fools. For instance, *Today, the monthly magazine of Scientific Socialism,* in its first issue of 1884 printed an article where it was taken for granted that "economically and socially Jews are our antagonists". This equation was not simply of Jews with capitalism. It was an equation of Jews with imperialist domination—a domination that was conscious and conspiratorial. *Justice,* the paper of the S.D.F., claimed that:

> **"Jew moneylenders now control every Foreign Office in Europe"**
> (5.4.1884)

and that:

> **"It seems to be an open secret that the government of France is too much in the grip of Jews to take active measures against them as a body"** (25.6.1898).

This latter quote was taken from the time of the Dreyfus affair in France. Similarly, Robert Blatchford's journal, *The Clarion* (around which the Clarion Clubs were organised), quoted with approval the claim that:

> **"Modern imperialism is really run by half a dozen financial houses, many of them Jewish, to whom politics is a counter in the game of buying and selling securities and the people are convenient pawns."** (24.2.1900)

It was frequently alleged that all imperialist wars were organised and manipulated by Jews, in the interest of Jewish finance. Sometimes it was suggested that this was channelled through just one family—the Rothschilds. *Labour Leader,* the paper of the I.L.P., stated that:

> **"Wherever there is trouble in Europe, wherever rumours of war circulate and men's minds are distraught with fear of change and calamity, you may be sure that a hooked-nosed Rothschild is at his games somewhee near the region of the disturbances"**
> (19.12.1891).

In particular, the Boer War and the events leading up to it were frequently pictured as being in defence of Jewish financial interests in South Africa. H.M. Hyndman, the leader of the S.D.F., warned against the construction of an

> **"Anglo-Hebraic empire in Africa"** (*Justice,* 25.4.1896).

Not only did Jews allegedly control the world through financial and military domination—but also, apparently, through control of the media. *Justice* spoke of supposed Jewish press power in England acting

> **"in accord with their fellow capitalist Jews all over the world"**
> (5.7.1890).

# Immigration Controls—The Acid Test

The **Aliens Act** of 1905 is almost entirely forgotten today by the Jewish community and by socialists. It was the natural corollary to the anti-Jewish ideology described above, namely the successful demand for immigration control on Jews. The Act was passed by a Tory government with the full support of its leadership and of the Tory Party. It was enforced by a Liberal government. However, in many ways it was the result of nearly twenty years of agitation by the English working class.

This agitation took two main forms. Firstly, there was the grassroots proto-fascist organisation in London's East End—the British Brothers League. Between its inception in 1901 and its victory in 1905, the Brothers organised constant demonstrations and rallies through the East End against Jewish immigration. Secondly, there was the organised labour movement itself. From 1892, the T.U.C. was formally committed to a resolution excluding Jews. This was not a passive 'paper' position, indeed the issue of immigration control was included in a list of questions to be asked of all Parliamentary candidates, which was compiled by a special conference of the T.U.C. in 1895 (*Manchester Evening News, 11.7.1895*). Indeed, the T.U.C. sent a delegation to the Home Secretary demanding control (*Times, 6.2.1896*).

This was only the tip of the iceberg. W.H. Wilkins, a fanatical campaigner for control, in his book *The Alien Invasion*, published in 1892, named 43 labour organisations, not including the T.U.C., advocating restrictions on Jews. These ranged from the National Boiler Makers and Iron Ship Builders Society to the Miners Association of Durham to the Oldham Provincial Card and Blowing Room Operatives. It also included the Liverpool Trades' Council. Many other trades' councils were to come out in favour of control. These included London, where control was supported by the renowned rank and file dockers' leaders Ben Tillett and Tom Mann (*London Evening News*, May 27th. and June 19th. 1891), Manchester (*Trades Council Report*, 1892) and Leeds (evidence of its secretary, to the 1903 *Royal Commission on Alien Immigration*). J.H. Wilson, who was an M.P. and also secretary of the Seamans' Union, was actually one of the first to propose legislation in Parliament (*Hansard, 11.2.1893*).

The attitude of most of the emergent socialist organisations to all of this, varied from agreement to inconsistency. For instance, *The Clarion* came out eventually for total exclusion. In an article just after

the Act became law, *The Clarion* stated that Jewish immigrants were:
> **"a poison injected into the national veins"**, they were the **"unsavoury children of the ghetto"**, their numbers were **"appalling"** and their attitudes **"unclean"** (22.6.1906).

The S.D.F.'s position was, to put it mildly, fainthearted. Hyndman at a meeting called ostensibly to oppose controls, declared that he was against **"free admittance of all aliens"** and went on to attack Jews for living in ghettos and refusing to intermarry (*Jewish Chronicle*, 1.4.1904).

## English and Jewish Opposition to Controls

Fortunately for the communist movement today, there is an alternative socialist tradition in relation to the Aliens Act from which we can learn. There **were** pockets of protest against the agitation for immigration control from within the emergent socialist movement and, to an even lesser extent, from within the labour movement as a whole. However, such protest was relatively small and could not swim against the tide. The most honourable example of this was the Socialist League, which split from the S.D.F. in 1885, and whose most well-remembered figure is William Morris. The League's journal, *Commonweal,* showed a totally principled position in its opposition to anti-semitism and immigration control. In one article—sarcastically called **"Blarsted Furriners"**—the journal attacked the other Left groups for their chauvinism and anti-semitism, asking them:

> **"Are we then to allow the issues at stake in the struggle between the robbers and the robbed to be obscured by anti-foreigner agitation?"** (28.4.1888).

The same article also then offered solidarity to the Aborigines, Maoris, American Indians and black people everywhere, against their exploitation by the colonising English. In another article, John Burns of the I.L.P. was criticised for claiming that **"England was for the English"** (23.8.1890). However, the League and its journal ceased to exist in the early 1890's—unable and unwilling to compete with the increasing chauvinism of its rival organisation. Nonetheless, individuals and individual branches within the **S.D.F.** and **I.L.P.** occasionally kept the torch of protest alight. Again, individual trades unionists occasionally tried to speak out. Thus there was some opposition on the London Trades Council to Tillett and Mann—Mr. Taylor (a lithographic artist) spoke out against restriction and in favour of the **"solidarity of the workers international brotherhood"** (*London Evening News* 19.6.1891).

It must be said, that with the honourable and important exceptions of the Socialist League and odd individuals, the remaining opposition to immigration control by the English socialist and labour movement was not only spasmodic, but was despite itself, and was the result of pressure put on it by its Jewish members. This was certainly the case with the S.D.F.—where it was essentially only its London East end branch (that is, its Jewish branch) which organised activity against the Act. In May 1904, the East London S.D.F. convened a conference composed of "delegates from the Jewish trade unions and others" to plan some disruption of Parliament over the proposed Act (*Jewish Chronicle* 6.5.1904). After the Act became law the East London S.D.F. organised a meeting of protest in the Wonderland, Whitechapel Rd. The meeting was conducted in Yiddish and English (*Jewish Chronicle,* 19.9.1905). In fact the S.D.F. meeting, where Hyndman had turned up and spoken in favour of control, had been organised by its East London branch as a meeting against control. Likewise, the I.L.P. held protests—but again apparently only through the pressure of its Jewish members. *Labour Leader* reported a protest meeting in Tib Street in Manchester and advised those who wanted to follow up the protest to get in touch with the I.L.P. through J. Deschman, who was secretary of the Jewish Tailors Union in Manchester (3.6.1904).

The only organised trade union opposition which included British trade unionists, was when Jewish workers took the initiative. The major examples of this was the meeting attended by over 3,000 people, organised in the East End by the Federated Jewish Tailors Union of London, where the speakes included W.P. Reeves of the Women's Union League, Margaret Bondfield, secretary of the National Union of Shop Assistants and Frank Brien of the Dockers Union (*Eastern Post,* 20.9.1902). The way in which at least some English workers were forced into action against anti-semitism by the independent initiative of Jewish workers is obviously mirrored today, when women and black organisation have placed sexism and racism on the political agenda of the Left.

Given the backward role of most of the English labour and socialist organisations, Jewish workers were compelled to take independent action against the agitation for immigrant control. An Alien Defence League was established by Jews to fight control and was

# A VOICE FROM THE ALIENS

## About the Anti-Alien Resolution of the Cardiff Trade Union Congress.

WE, the organised Jewish workers of England, taking into consideration the Anti-Alien Resolution, and the uncomplimentary remarks of certain delegates about the Jewish workers specially, issue this leaflet, wherewith we hope to convince our English fellow workers of the untruthfulness, unreasonableness, and want of logic contained in the cry against the foreign worker in general, and against the Jewish worker in particular.

It is, and always has been, the policy of the ruling classes to attribute the sufferings and miseries of the masses (which are natural consequences of class rule and class exploitation) to all sorts of causes except the real ones. The cry against the foreigner is not merely peculiar to England ; it is international. Everywhere he is the scapegoat for other's sins. Every class finds in him an enemy. So long as the Anti-Alien sentiment in this country was confined to politicians, wire-pullers, and to individual working men, we, the organised aliens, took no heed ; but when this ill-founded sentiment has been officially expressed by the organised working men of England, then we believe that it is time to lift our voices and argue the matter out.

It has been proved by great political economists that a working man in a country where machinery is greatly developed produces in a day twice as many commodities as his daily wage enables him to consume.

*A pamphlet produced by Jewish Trades Unionists, in opposition to the 1905 Aliens Act.*

based at 38 Brick Lane in London (*Jewish Chronicle*, 24.1.1902). Moreover, Jewish trade unionists took initiatives that were directed specifically against the anti-semitism of the English labour movement. In 1895, Jewish trade unionists in London circulated a leaflet called *The Voice of the Alien* which attacked the T.U.C.'s support for immigration control. This was written by Joseph Finn, a Jewish socialist from Leeds (see his letter to the *Jewish Chronicle*, 14.2.1902). Alongside this, *Der Arbeiter Freund* (The Worker's Friend, a Yiddish anarcho-communist journal) consistently attacked the English labour movement for its chauvinism and anti-semitism. It correctly understood the alignment of forces when it attacked the T.U.C. and **"its papa—the State"** (17.4.1903 quoted in *Immigrants and the Class Struggle* by Joe Buckman).

It could be argued that this Jewish fight-back, within and against the English labour movement, did have some limited success, in that one or two trade unions did alter their position. Thus, by 1903, Manchester Trades Council had become simply indifferent to the question of control and had ceased to campaign for it (*Manchester Evening News*, 28.1.1903). A similar neutralisation occurred with respect to Leeds Trades Council. Again, in 1905, James Sexton, the President of the T.U.C. personally denounced control at the T.U.C. conference (1905 T.U.C. Annual Report).

In conclusion, there are two points which can be made. Firstly, it was all far too little and too late. Only one or two labour movement bodies actually stopped campaigning for control. The T.U.C. was not one of these. No organised union body ever campaigned against control. In any event, after 1901 the working class movement for control had taken to the streets with a vengeance, under the leadership of the British Brothers League. Secondly, insofar as one or two union organisations **did** ameliorate their position, it was more due to the (belated) recognition that the militancy and high degree of unionisation of Jewish workers were actually helping raise the living standards of English workers than the result of Jewish opposition to control. For instance, Tom Mann and Ben Tillett were prepared to speak at the inaugural meeting of the Federation of East London Labour Unions in 1889. G. Kelley, secretary of the Manchester Trades Council, explaining why the Council no longer supported control, emphasised the good example that the Jewish Tailors Union in Manchester had set for English workers (*Manchester Evening News*, 28.1.1903). In other words, even this small group of labour orga-

# UNITY, FRATERNITY & STRENGTH!

Under the auspices of the
HEBREW CABINET MAKERS' SOCIETY, STICK AND CANE DRESSERS' UNION,
INTERNATIONAL FURRIERS' SOCIETY,
TAILOR-MACHINISTS' UNION, TAILORS' AND PRESSERS' UNION,
AMALGAMATED LASTERS' SOCIETY, UNITED CAPMAKERS' SOCIETY, AND
INTERNATIONAL JOURNEYMAN BOOT-FINISHERS' SOCIETY,

A

# Mass Meeting

will take place on
## SATURDAY, DECEMBER 28th, 1889,
at the
## GREAT ASSEMBLY HALL
### MILE END ROAD, E.

## To inaugurate the Federation of East-London Labour Unions.

The Chair will be taken at 3 p.m. prompt by
## Mr. CHARLES V. ADAMS,
Who will be supported by the following speakers: Messrs.
**J. MACDONALD, TOM WALKER, J. TURNER,
TOM MANN, BEN TILLETT,
H. SPARLING, H. DAVIS, C. MOWBRAY,**
Mrs. SCHACK, WESS, WEINBERG, FEIGENBAUM,
ROCHMAN, M. FRENCHMAN, L. COHEN, LIGHTMAN,
SKITTEN, ROSENBERG, GOLDSTEIN, SEBERSKY,
LEEK, and GOLDSTONE.

All members of the above unions are earnestly requested to attend this
most important meeting.

## WORKERS OF THE WORLD UNITE!

Communications in connection with the above to be addressed to the Hon. Sec.
W. WESS, 12, Clark St. Bedford Sq. E.

א גרויסע
# מאסטע פֿעראָאמלונ
פֿעראַנשטאלטעט פֿון אללע אידישע אַרבייטער פֿעראײנען,
וועט שטאטטונדען
שבת. דין 28-טען דעצעמבער, אם 3 אהר נאכמיטטאג, אין דיא
גרייט אססעמבלי האלל, מייל ענד ראוד,
אום צו פֿיערין דיא גרינדונג פֿון דיא פֿעדעריישאן פֿון אללע ארבייטער פֿעראײנען

*Tom Mann and Ben Tillett speak at the meeting to inaugurate the Federation of East London Labour Unions—Jews can be supported as trades unionists, but not as "aliens"!*

26

nisation did not renounce anti-semitism. Rather they concealed it behind a newly discovered economic identification with Jewish workers.

## Rich Jew, Poor Jew—The Conspiracy Theory in Practice

Arguments often used in favour of control were that Jewish workers were taking away English people's jobs, undercutting wages, weakening unionisation and taking away housing from the English. An obvious question that arises is the connection between an anti-semitic movement which was directed against working class Jews, and the anti-semitic notion of Jewish capitalist domination. Of course, there could be no rational connection, but given assumptions about the world Jewish conspiracy, then links could be made on the most irrational and transcendental of levels.

One way of dealing with this was to try and make some distinction between "rich Jews" and "poor Jews". It is at this point some of the socialists' apparent opposition to control becomes quite ambiguous, as opposition was also couched in anti-semitic imagery. For instance, in 1904 the I.L.P. actually issued a pamphlet against control—*The Problem of Alien Immigration*. On its first page it mounted an attack on:

> **"The rich Jew who has done his best to besmirch the fair name of England and to corrupt the sweetness of our national life and character"**

and to compare this to the **"poor Jew"** who should be allowed in.

More frequently, the socialist groups tried to discover actual links between "rich Jews" and "poor Jews", in order to attack the latter as being in some way a pawn of the former. For instance, Beatrice Potter, one of the founders of the Fabians, constantly argued in her investigation of East End life that the only aim of a Jewish worker was to become a capitalist. In one essay she wrote that:

> **"The love of profit distinct from other forms of money earning"**
> is **"the strongest impelling motive of the Jewish race"**
> *Nineteenth Century, vol XXIV*).

This is not so much a picture of the poor Jew as pawn, but rather of the poor Jew as embryonic capitalist, clone and biological imperialist. The Fabians, as an organisation, never opposed control—they merely abstained and let it happen. Moreover, Beatrice Potter deliberately lied about Jews in the East End by concealing all reference to the powerful Jewish labour movement developing there. Indeed, in the essay quoted above, she claims that Jews, as embryonic capitalists:

**"Have neither the desire nor the capacity for labour combination".**

Potter combined very well the prejudices of the attack on rich Jews and on poor Jews.

Ben Tillett had another angle. He argued that it was ultimately the British government which was a pawn in the hands of Jewish capitalists and was therefore reluctant to enact controls. He asserted:

**"Our leading statesmen do not care to offend the great banking houses or money kings"**

and went on to say:

**"For heaven's sake, give us back our own countrymen and take from us your motley multitude"**

(*London Evening News*, 19.6.1891).

So it seems, Tillett perceived Jewish financiers—**"money kings"**—as somehow engineering and manipulating the immigration of the Jewish masses—**"your motley multitude"**. Tillett was quite willing to speak on the same platform as the most infamous Jew baiters, none of whom cared whether Jews were rich or poor. He spoke on the same platform as Arnold White at a meeting of an early control organisation—The Association for Preventing the Immigration of Destitute Aliens (*London Evening News and Post*, 25.7.1891). At this meeting he was supported by J.H. Wilson of the Sailor's Union, J. Tanter of the Progressive Union of Cabinetmakers, J. Cross of the St. Helens Colliery Enginemen's Society and "many other delegates from trade unions in London and the country". In 1900, at the T.U.C. Conference, a new dimension was introduced when John Ward, leader of the Navvies' Union argued that:

**"Practically £100,000 of the taxpayer's money has been spent in trying to secure the gold fields of South Africa for cosmopolitan Jews, most of whom had no patriotism and no country"** (*T.U.C. Annual Report*, 1900).

In other words, all Jews, rich or poor, were cosmopolitan with gold on their mind—particularly South African gold.

It is relevant to note another way the conspiracy theory operated. Whilst "socialists" were attacking Jews as either imperialist financiers or lumpen scabs, the bourgeoisie were attacking them as militant

28

trade unionists and anarchists. The *London Evening News* proclaimed that:

> **"The advance of socialistic and anarchical opinion in London is commensurate with the increased volume of foreign immigration"** (21.5.1891).

Given the conspiracy theory, the bourgeoisie had no need even for themselves to be consistent about this. So S.H. Jeyes, another ardent restrictionist, argued in his essay *Foreign Pauper Immigration* In A. White (Ed.) *The Destitute Alien of Great Britain* that Jews deliberately did not organise in unions, in order to suppress the general level of wages, and so incite the English to revolution. As he put it:

> **"To strengthen the spirit of discontent and disorder on which the agitators live and batten and which in time would pollute England with the visionary violence of continental socialism"**.

Finally, in this context of the conspiracy theory in action, it is worth noting that the British Brothers League attracted members who regarded themselves as socialists. At least one member of the Independant Labour Party left that organisation to join the Brothers (*The Eastern Post* 19.10.1901). Someone signing themselves "Mile End Socialist" wrote to the *Jewish Chronicle* (21.11.1902) stating that:

> **"'Jew versus Gentile' will be my battle cry at every election as long as life is spared... the Jew has made himself obnoxious through the incarnate instinct of his race to every nation where he has now emigrated. This is an historical fact and beyond controversy"**.

## Anti-Alienism or Anti-Semitism?

Bourgeois historians—and these are the only historians who have hitheto examined this subject—have argued that the struggle for the Aliens Act was based on xenophobia against **all** foreigners rather than on anti-semitism. Colin Holmes in his book *Anti-Semitism in British Society* argues that:

> **"It is more important to categorise the 1905 Act as anti-alien rather than anti-semitic"**

and that:

> **"The legislation was aimed at aliens rather than specifically at Jews as Jews"**.

According to this viewpoint, it was just bad luck and coincidence that Jews were restricted—it could have been any foreigner. Now this attempt to deny the specificity of immigration controls is extremely reactionary. Exactly the same argument is used in relation to the current Immigration Act—where attempts are constantly being made to deny its specific anti-black racism by the assertion that it keeps out all foreigners. As socialists we should oppose all immigration controls. This is precisely because any immigration control is inevitably based on national chauvinism—namely the belief that foreigners are in some way inferior to the English. It is crucial to appreciate the political dimension of controls, that they are never brought in against the whole world, in the abstract, but are always brought in against a specific non-English victim group, through the use of specific imageries.

Obviously, one aspect of the movement for the Aliens Act was a generalised chauvinism against all foreigners. England is the imperialist country par excellence and therefore popular ideology is inevitably chauvinistic. Many examples of this can be found within the early socialist movements. Bruce Glasier of the I.L.P. argued in *Labour Leader* that:

**"Neither the principle of the brotherhood of man nor the principle of social equality implies that brother nations or brother men may crowd upon us in such numbers as to abuse our hospitality, overturn our institutions or violate our customs"** (3.4.1904).

Such phrases as "our institutions" clearly substitute a chauvinistic analysis for a class one.

However, it is inadequate to regard the Aliens Act as being simply based on such general chauvinism against all-comers. This underestimates the strength of anti-semitism and misunderstands the history of immigration control—and thus fails to understand the real relationship between the two. The Aliens Act was aimed specifically at Jews by invoking specifically anti-semitic imagery. In essence, running right through the movement for control, were variants of the theory of the world Jewish conspiracy. Moreover, much of the actual imagery used by 'socialists' was of the basest anti-semitic kind— harking back to medieval Christianity and looking forward to Nazism. The frequent reference in *The Clarion* to Jews as **"The nose"** (1.9.1892) is not a trivial example. Again, much of the language used to describe alleged Jewish capitalist domination was itself of a classic anti-semitic mould. A.J. Hobson's writings are typical. Hobson was a well-known radical journalist of the day, who later became prominent in the Labour Party and made his name covering the Boer War as a journalist for the Manchester Guardian. It was his opinion that the Transvaal was controlled by **"Jew power"** and

> **"those who came early made most and then left leaving their economic fangs in the carcase of their pray"** (*Contemporary Review* vol LXXVII).

The image of the Jew as parasite and bloodsucker is an historical constant within anti-semitism.

The history of immigration control, itself, illustrates the nonsense of regarding the 1905 legislation as being simply the product of an anti-alienism, to which anti-semitism was peripheral. The significant point is that prior to 1905 England had never had serious immigration control (at least since the explusion of the Jews by Edward 1st). Today, it is difficult to appreciate that a century ago immigration control was a novel concept, and it needed the struggle against the Jews to legitimise it. Even this required a prolonged struggle which lasted nearly two decades—1885 to 1905. A comparison between the response to Jews and to other immigrants is illuminating. Irish immigration into England throughout the 19th century was greeted with almost total hostility. Anti-Irish chauvinism was as enormous as it is today. In one way, the Irish were even more vulnerable than the Jews—their own country had been devastated and colonised by the English. But whatever else it did, the agitation against the Irish did not lead to immigration control.

Similarly, at the same time as agitating against Jews, some parts of the labour movement were agitating for controls against non-Jewish workers. For instance, Keir Hardie, a founder member of the I.L.P., gave evidence at the 1889 House of Commons Select Committee on Immigration. He spoke on behalf of the Ayrshire Miners Union and the Scottish Labour Party. As well as opposing Jewish immigration— save for those fleeing persecution—these organisations were opposed to Polish Christians being allowed to come and work in the mines, in iron and steel mills and on British ships. The essential objection to this was the importation of scab labour to work these industries in times of industrial unrest. However, no legislation was ever introduced against immigrant strike-breakers. This was in spite of the fact that Hardie, who incidentally himself voted against the Act, introduced an amendment to the Aliens Bill calling for the exclusion of immigrant strike-breakers. In the end the only controls enacted were those which were aimed at Jews.

Of course, particular reasons can be advanced as to why the

bourgeoisie did not exclude other groups. They had no material interest in excluding scab labour and they **did** have a material interest in the use of manual Irish labour. Moreover, if one were to look at the matter purely from the point of view of imperialist material self-interest, then the bourgeoisie should not have included the Jews—as Jews organised whole sections of the garment and footwear industries. However, such an economically deterministic approach to history simply ignores the role of ideology as a factor in politics.

Thus it was anti-semitism which was the ingredient necessary to popularise the ideology of immigration control, so that such control became politically viable. This is no coincidence and relates in part to the nature of anti-semitism. All movements for control against any foreigner invoke the image of the alien horde taking over Britain. What distinguished anti-Jewish agitation was the conspiracy theory. This asserted that the Jew had a conscious plan to take over, not simply Britain, but the entire world. This was an extremely comprehensive and therefore powerful justification for control. In the end it was irresistable. In other words anti-semitism, far from being simply an example of, or peripheral to, anti-alienism, was the force which ensured anti-alienism would be given statutory authority for the first time.

The legitimisation of immigration control has had enormous repercussions in the 20th. century, not least because it kept out tens of thousands of Jews from England in the 1930's—thus resulting in their deaths. It also meant that the equally racist agitation for controls against black people was successful, in a relatively rapid period. It took just four years after the race attacks in 1958 in Notting Hill and Nottingham, before control was legislated. The labour movement did not campaign either for or against it: controls were accepted as "natural" and being based on "common sense". It was the active, if forgotten, struggle for controls by the labour movement over 60 years earlier, which had legitimised them.

## Imperialism and History

Socialists, Marx in particular, correctly emphasise the need for a consciousness of history, so that we may learn from it. However, socialist historians have simply ignored the Aliens Act which has led to a serious gap in the understanding, not just of anti-semitism, but of imperialism. It is obviously not possible to appreciate the history of immigration controls without understanding the Aliens Act, nor is it possible to understand how false ideology penetrated both the trade union movement and large sections of the early socialist movement. Indeed the struggle for immigration controls against Jews is a classic example of how imperialism, particularly English imperialism, works in practice. It is a crystal clear instance of how the English ruling class repeatedly attacks immigrant masses, whether they be Jewish, Irish or black—through an alliance not only with the English masses but through attempted alliances with the leaders of the immigrant community. Hence there were three major social forces which were attacking the Jews.

The first such force was the English bourgeoisie who won English workers away from their class interests by the false consciousness of 'national interests'. The Prime Minister of the Tory government which passed the Aliens Act was Arthur Balfour. Balfour is regarded by zionists as a major friend of the Jewish people as it was his Declaration in 1917 that promised a Jewish 'national home' in Palestine. To regard Balfour as a friend of the Jewish people reveals much about zionist philosophy. Balfour was an anti-semite who wanted to exclude Jews from England on the grounds that, as he stated in the 1905 debate on the Aliens Act, Jews were not

**"to the advantage of the civilisation of this country"** and

**"they are a people apart and not only hold a religion differing from the vast majority of their fellow countrymen but only intermarry amongst themselves".**

Again, Joseph Chamberlain M.P. is well known in history books for his 'social imperialism'. This was his attempt to win British workers over to imperialism by offering social reforms. He is famous for his unsuccessful campaign for protectionism and import controls against 'foreign' goods but there seems to be little knowledge that he combined this with propaganda for 'Jew controls'. Moreover, the Liberal government of 1906, combining as it did massive social reforms with the enforcement of immigration controls against Jewish people, is a variant of social imperialism.

Exactly the same can be said about the post-1945 welfare state and about the ideology of 'welfarism' itself: it combined social reforms with increasing immigration controls against black people. The battle for these politics had been won decades earlier over the struggle for the Aliens Act. The welfare state has now taken this one stage further against black people through the implementation of internal controls by the Home Office or by the 'caring' agencies of the state who assess entitlement to welfare benefits through the criteria of nationality and residence.

The second element in the attack on the Jewish masses was the Jewish establishment, who were won over by the British ruling class. The Jewish communal leadership in this country did not immigrate here as an already formed block, but was created through its treacherous alliance with the British bourgeoisie. Class interest was stronger than any 'communal' interest. The Jewish establishment policed the Jewish masses on behalf of the British ruling class, by pressurising them into assimilation and anglicisation. Moreover, major sections of the Jewish leadership actually advocated immigration control.

Benjamin Cohen was an M.P. and President of the Jewish Board of Guardians. In 1894 he told the annual general meeting of the Board that:

> **"Jews should make it clear not to endeavour to oppose any action which the responsible advisors to the Crown may deem necessary for the national interests which we are as desirous to protect as our fellow citizens"**

(quoted by Gartner in *The Jewish Immigrant in Britain*).

Cohen was created a Baronet in the Resignation Honours of 1905, immediately after voting for the Aliens Act. Harry Samuels, another Jewish M.P., spoke on the same platform as the British Brothers League, at a rally organised by them in the East End which attracted an audience of 4,000 (*East London Observer*, 18.1.1902). Samuels declared his **"intention to discharge his duties as an English citizen"**. Also speaking at this meeting was Arnold White—who manifestly regarded Jewish Tory M.P.'s like Samuels, and British trade union militants, such as Tillett, as equal allies in his restrictionist crusade.

Actually, the Jewish establishment did not need the Aliens Act—it was quite prepared to use its own initiative and send Jews back to Russia and to further pogroms. Lionel Alexander, Secretary to the Board of Guardians, told the House of Commons Select Committee on Immigration in 1888 that:

> **"My Board does not favour unwarranted immigration but do their utmost to check it by warnings rather than prohibitions... it is one of our largest operations sending people back who, having wandered here, prove useless".**

In other words, a section of the Jewish leadership was prepared to do the dirty work for the British ruling class and to police the Jewish community as an alternative to legislative control.

Of course some elements of the Jewish bourgeoisie did take a principled opposition to the demand for control and the anti-semitism that stimulated it. However, this was tiny. There were few communal organisations that came out in opposition, and those which did were reluctant and only acted under pressure of the Jewish masses. It took the *Jewish Chronicle* until a few weeks before the Act became law to recognise the strength of grassroots Jewish opposition and to suggest that it might be amended through a 'write-in' campaign to Members of Parliament (*Jewish Chronicle*, 9.6.1905). Propelled by the activities of Jewish workers, this obviously fell well short of what was required.

The third element in this story is the role of the English working class. This is the concern of the present book. It is undeniable that the working class played an important role in the agitation for controls; it is arguable that without their intervention controls would not have been introduced. Certainly, the campaigning of the organised labour movement and the British Brothers League was far in excess of the demagogy of the bourgeois politicians and their press. It was as though the working class agitation assumed a relative autonomy of its own. Behind this, 'socialist' groups such as the S.D.F. and the I.L.P. provided false rationalisations. All this is important today—not least because the present Labour Party was constituted precisely on trade union affiliation and was supported by organisations such as the I.L.P. and the Fabians.

## Fascists Reclaim History

At its best, the Left ignores the history of anti-semitism and therefore of imperialism within the labour movement. At its worst, it is even prepared to rewrite history. An example of this is the quaintly titled pamphlet *"Zionism..., anti-semitism's twin in Jewish Garb"*. by Tony Greenstein and produced by Brighton Labour Briefing (a grouping within Brighton Labour Party). In its opening paragraph it makes the incredible assertion that zionism exploited **"the natural hatred of the labour movement for anti-semitism"**. It is as though the political agitation by the trade union movement, which was anti-semitic to the core and supported by many socialists, to keep Jews out just did not happen. The labour movement is now claimed to be 'naturally' (whatever that means) opposed to anti-semitism.

35

This ignorance and dishonesty does itself have political consequences. Groupings within the fascist movement today have an acute awareness of the history of early socialism—and embrace this history as their own! For instance there was an article in the National Front magazine, *Spearhead,* in March 1980 called 'Nationalism and the Old British Socialists'. This was produced at a time when a faction of the N.F., led by Martin Webster, was arguing that the organisation had to have a working class base with the politics of 'national socialism'. With justification, this article could claim that such a tradition already existed. *Spearhead* began by stating:

> **"Modern socialists who support the so-called 'Anti Nazi League' and other anti-racialist organisations would be highly embarrassed to learn of the nationalist and racialist attitudes displayed by many early British socialists".**

The article then praised particular groups and individuals— Robert Blatchford's Clarion Clubs, the Fabians, the S.D.F., the I.L.P. and various trade unionists. Blatchford's book *Merrie England,* which combined the demand for import controls with virulent anti-semitism, was said to be

> **"echoed by the Nationalist Movement which blossomed all over Europe in the 1920's and 30's".**

The Fabians, Beatrice Potter and Sydney Webb, were praised for describing Jews in the book *Industrial Democracy* as a **"constant influence for degradation"** and George Bernard Shaw for characterising the Jews as

> **"the real enemy, the invader from the East, the Druze, the ruffian, the oriental parasite"** (*Morning Post,* 13.12.25).

Pete Curran, a leading member of the Gasworkers Union and the I.L.P. was approved for advocating controls against Jews. Hyndman of the S.D.F. was claimed as the first National Socialist. The article ends by stating:

> **"The obvious patriotism and candid racialism of these early socialists is in marked contrast to the attitudes and views held by socialists today. The triumph of internationalism and the changes from an open-minded and well-meaning approach to a mindless religious fanaticism is a reflection of the changing genetic complexion of Socialism's own advocates".**

Presumably the 'changing genetic complexion' means that Jews are now supposedly controlling the Left, as well as everything else. The reality is that anti-semitism still exists today on the Left. One aspect is the refusal even to acknowledge the anti-semitism of much of our own tradition. Unless, as socialists, we undertake this re-evaluation, then we are ideologically powerless to prevent fascists embracing the anti-semitism of our history.

# TO TAILORS AND TAILORESSES !!!

## GREAT

# STRIKE

of

# LONDON TAILORS

## & SWEATER'S VICTIMS.

FELLOW WORKERS,

You are all aware that a Commission of Lords have been appointed to enquire into the evils of the Sweating System in the Tailoring Trade. The Revelations made before the Commission by Witnesses engaged in the Tailoring Trade, are a Disgrace to a Civilised Country. The Sweaters' Victims had hoped that this Commission, would have come to some satisfactory conclusion as to an alteration in the condition of the Sweated Tailors. Finding they have just put off their deliberation until Next Session, we have decided to take Immediate Action.

It is too long for us to wait, until Next Session, because the hardships inflicted upon us by the Sweater are unbearable. We have therefore decided to join in the GENERAL DEMAND FOR INCREASED COMFORT AND SHORTER HOURS OF LABOUR. Our Hours at present being on an average from 14 to 18 per day, in unhealthy and dirty dens.

WE DEMAND:

(1) THAT THE HOURS BE REDUCED TO 12 WITH AN INTERVAL OF ONE HOUR FOR DINNER AND HALF-HOUR FOR TEA.

(2) ALL MEALS TO BE HAD OFF THE PREMISES.

(3) GOVERNMENT CONTRACTORS TO PAY WAGES AT TRADE UNION RATES.

(4) GOVERNMENT CONTRACTORS AND SWEATERS NOT TO GIVE WORK HOME AT NIGHT AFTER WORKING HOURS.

We now Appeal for the support of all Tailors to join us and thus enable us to Successfully Enforce our Demands, which are reasonable,

## Tailors & Tailoresses support in joining this General Strike.

We Appeal to all Tailors, Machinists, Pressers, Basters, &c. to meet, EN-MASSE, on THURSDAY, FRIDAY & SATURDAY MORNINGS, at 10 o'clock, (outside the Baths) GOULSTON STREET, WHITECHAPEL. E.

### Piece Workers Finish Up, Week Workers Give Notice at Once,

ALL WORK TO CEASE ON SATURDAY AFTERNOON WHEN THE STRIKE WILL BE DECLARED.

Signed, STRIKE COMMITTEE,

| | | | M. Rosenthall, |
| Lewis Lyons, Chairman | Richard Roskeli;". | Annie Goodman, | Jacob Sydler, | Harris Frank |
| J. Green | Phillip White, | L. Goldstein, | J. Margolis, | Lewis Perlburg, |
| J. Silverman | Simon Cohen | Charles Mowbray, | D. Greenbaum | W. Wess, Secretary. |

Tailors Strike Committee Room "White Hart," Greenfield-st., Commercial-Rd. All communications to be addressed to the Secty

P.S. We appeal to those engaged in the Trade to at once join either of the following Societies:
"JEWISH BRANCH, AMALGAMATED SOCIETY OF TAILORS," Meets on Sunday Evenings, from 8 till 10, at the " White Hart," Greenfield Street, Commercial Road, E.
"PRESSERS SOCIETY," Meet Sunday Evenings, from 8 till 10, at the " Man in the Moon," Plough Street, Commercial Road, E.
"MANTEL MAKERS, TAILORS AND MACHINISTS SOCIETY " Meet Saturday Evenings, from 7 till 10 at the " White Hart," Greenfield Street, Commercial Road, E.

AUGUST 27th, 1889

T. G. SAWYER, PRINTER, 227, BETHNAL GREEN ROAD

*Poster for Tailors and Tailoresses Strike of 1889.*

# The Left Returns to Zion

## The Left Organisations

It would be surprising if the anti-semitism which flourished within the English socialist tradition at its formation had simply disappeared. False consciousness has to be challenged—and there was little opposition to the socialism of fools. Today, however, it has assumed a very different form. Rather than the caricature of the Jew as all-powerful capitalist, there is now the frequent equation of zionism with world domination and of all Jews being zionists, or at least responsible for zionism. This equation can be found in an explicit form within the Stalinist tradition. A classic case was the intended show trial, cancelled in the wake of Stalin's death, of the five 'Jewish doctors' from the Kremlin's own hospital, who were accused in 1953 of attempting, under 'zionist influence', to poison Stalin and most of the communist hierarchy. Similarly, in Poland today, the regime has attacked both Solidarity and K.O.R. (the intellectual group influential with Solidarity) as being controlled by a 'zionist clique'. Two articles by Zbigniew Kot in the paper of the Polish communist party— described K.O.R. as having the:

**"Pseudo-left programme of the Trotskyite International which is inspired by zionist circles"**

and:

**"K.O.R. openly confesses to having sympathies for free-masonry and for the cosmopolitan fatherland-negating concepts promoted in the West by zionist and free-thinking circles".**

(*Trybuna Ludu*, 22/23.12.81 quoted in *Research Report of the Institute of Jewish Affairs* May 1982).

Anti-semitism posing as anti-zionism is particularly frightening within Stalinism, as Stalinism has state power in many countries. It occurs sometimes in a confused and sometimes in an unambiguous way, in the new Left groups consolidated since the 1960's in this country. Attitudes within the Labour Party are far more complex for various reasons. Firstly, given the coalition of interests within the Labour Party, there is no guarantee that the leadership ever reflects the will of the Party. Secondly, the commonly-held belief that historically the Labour leadership has been pro-zionist, does itself need serious revision.

It is undoubtedly the case that the Labour Party has made many outspoken statements of sympathy for zionism. As early as December 1917, at a special conference of the Labour Party and the T.U.C. to draw up a 'was aims memorandum', it was acknowledged that Palestine was a land **"to which such of the Jewish people as desired to do so may return and work out their salvation"**.

In the following years numerous similar resolutions were passed. (See documents collected in *British Labour Policy on Palestine*, edited by Levenberg). Indeed Poale Zion, the pro-zionist Jewish workers party, has long been affiliated to the Labour Party, but it is simply a myth to regard the Labour leadership as having a genuine commitment to zionism. Ultimately, its position on the Middle East was, and is, guided by purely diplomatic considerations—that is by considerations of imperialism.

The Labour government of 1945 emulated the Tories in relation to Palestine as in India, by playing off the conflicting communal groups through false promises to both. Again, it was the same Labour government which mobilised the British army to prevent Jewish refugees fleeing to Palestine. Indeed in 1947, Labour ordered two destroyers to intercept the refugee boat Exodus on its way to Palestine with over 4000 Jews on board and forced it to divert to Germany. The rationale was that Germany was the

> **"only territory under British jurisdiction outside of Cyprus where such large numbers of people can be housed and fed at such short notice".** (*Palestine Post, 21.8.47*).

The Hamburg docks saw the survivors of Nazism being dragged by British soldiers back onto German soil.

Since the creation of Israel, Labour's politics have been determined solely by the need for imperialism to secure a base within the Middle East, and rationalised by a typically social democratic confusion that Israel is in some way a socialist state. At no time has the politics of the Labour Party ever been motivated by genuine commitment to the freedom of either the Jewish or the Arab masses. In a very real sense this is anti-semitism by default: there is no consideration of either the relationship , or lack of it, between zionism and Jewish liberation in Labour's attitude towards zionism.

The emphasis of the rest of this chapter is on the Trotskyist and neo-Trotskyist groups which constitute the New Left. Some of these, or at least their individual members, have in fact virtually dissolved themselves into the Labour Party. Of course such organisations are extremely small, but they represent a significant continuation of socialist politics following the degeneration of Stalinism. The New Left groups of today claim to be preserving the traditions of revolutionary socialism. This claim is in many positive ways justified. However, much of their purported anti-zionism rests on a tradition which, whatever the revolutionary rhetoric, has always been anti-semitic.

## The Issues

Any attempt at even a discussion of the relationship between anti-semitism and anti-zionism is normally calculated to cause apoplexy on the Left. This is no reason to censor the discussion, it is a reason for clarity and several points need to be clarified:

(1)  It would be patently absurd to regard all socialist writings antagonistic to zionism as being based on anti-semitism. The present book is not about zionism—but it is certainly hostile to it. Nathan Weinstock's book, *Zionism the False Messiah*, is a brilliant communist work. There are others. Anti-semitism is a relative not an absolute phenomenon on the Left.

(2)  It is not only absurd but reactionary to make a direct equation between anti-zionism and anti-semitism, on a theoretical level. The two are obviously not identical. Indeed it is grossly insulting to define the struggle of the Palestinians for liberation as being in any way intrinsically anti-semitic. It is similarly insulting to condemn as anti-semitic any solidarity with that struggle. It is a tragedy there is not more solidarity—there cannot be enough.

(3)  It is equally tragic that much of what passes for 'anti-zionism' on the Left is profoundly anti-semitic. It is a debatable point as to whether or not this is the dominant view on the Left. All that matters is that anti-semitism is now an important and legitimate tendancy within the Left. It is the existence of this tendency which allows the zionist leadership to condemn all Left critiques of zionism as being anti-Jewish. It feeds the anti-communism of

40

this reactionary leadership. The Left claims it makes a rigorous distinction between anti-zionism and anti-semitism yet it is manifestly not rigorous in practice. In practice, any condemnation by Jewish people of anti-semitism is somehow seen as an attempt to justify zionism.

(4) It is insufficient and unserious merely to assert that some, but not other, 'anti-zionist' politics are anti-semitic without distinguishing between a principled anti-zionism and anti-semitism. Without a scientific definition of anti-semitism the whole debate becomes useless and painful. In fact, anti-semitism in this context, as in every other context is rooted in a variant of the world Jewish conspiracy. This has two linked aspects in relation to notions of 'zionism': (a) the concept of zionism is expanded to equate it with world domination; (b) the entire Jewish experience is reduced to 'zionism' —and likewise all Jews are held to be responsible for zionism. This is the concept of collective guilt which is intrinsic to theories of the world conspiracy. It is the presence of these ideas which distinguishes anti-semitism from genuine anti-zionism.

(5) The distinction between anti-zionism and anti-semitism is absolute. Methodologically, there is no question of anti-zionism 'merging into' or 'becoming' anti-semitism. We are talking about two completely different phenomena. If an analysis is anti-semitic then it is anti-semitic in its origins and absolutely so—it does not become so. There is no such concept as anti-zionism 'tinged' with anti-semitism.

To take an example, Fascist organisations in this country are consistently anti-Israel. Issue number 15 of *Nationalism Today* (a National Front magazine) had an article attacking Israel and concluding with the exhortation—**"Anti-zionists of the world unite and fight!"** The September, 1982 issue of *Spearhead* (the private magazine of John Tyndall) had a three page supplement on **"The Jewish rape of Lebanon"**. The National Front even tried to infiltrate the first anniversary commemoration demonstration for the Sabra-Chatilla massacres. They had 'anti-zionist' leaflets. It would be grotesque to characterise groups like the National Front as 'anti-zionist'. They are anti-semitic plain and simple.

The starting point for genuine anti-zionism is full support for the Palestinian people in their struggle for liberation. This inevitably involves some analysis of the penetration of imperialism into the

Middle East and the undoubted role of Israel in furthering this. It also has to involve a recognition of the fact that zionism is itself an attempt by Jews to escape the scourge of anti-semitism, in a world where no other escape routes have become apparent. Conversely, the starting point for anti-semitism is the blaming of everything on Jews collectively and internationally—especially whatever happens in the Middle East. This is also its finishing point. The examples given below are **not** about solidarity with the Palestinians, but are about Jews—Jews everywhere. The attempt to expropriate the language of anti-zionism does not disguise the deep anti-semitism. These examples concern themselves not with zionism, but with Jews.

## Zionism and the Theory of World Domination

The equation of zionism with world domination shares a similar incoherence with the notion of the Jewish world conspiracy. It is unclear whether zionism is already supposed to have international power or whether it is still trying to achieve it via the Israeli state. The section that follows contains many examples.

A glaring example occurred in the paper of the Workers Revolutionary Party (*Newsline*, 8.12.79). This managed to combine the long-standing belief in international Jewish financial power with modern political zionism. The paper quoted with approval a member of the National Union of Mineworkers who said: **"It was Britain who sold the Palestinian people out to Zionist money power"**. The reference here is presumably to the period before 1948 when Britain was the Mandate authority ruling Palestine. One would have thought that a supposedly Marxist journal would at least have commented that Britain "sold out" the Palestinians because of Britain's imperialist interests. However, the quotation continues without comment as though it were from *Der Sturmer* (propaganda newspaper of the Nazi party in Germany), **"Many promises were made to the Palestinians but none were delivered for fear of upsetting the Jewish '£' sign"**. In fact, the sentiments behind this are remarkable similar to the "explanation" given by the National Front as to why the United States government allowed Israel to invade the Lebanon—**"because America's economy, mass media and political system is totally dominated by the Zionist-Jewish Money Power"**. (*National Front News*, August 1982).

*Newsline* has in fact managed to reproduce the notion of the media as under zionist influence—a typical instance of the conspiracy theory. In March 1983, the B.B.C. "Money Programme" purported to show that the W.R.P. was financed by the Libyan regime. One response to this by *Newsline* was an editorial which claimed that the programme was **"zionist sponsored"** (9.4.83). The same editorial then pointed out that Stuart Young had recently been appointed chairman of the B.B.C. Young was described as being a director of the *Jewish Chronicle*. No explanation was given of the politics of the *Jewish Chronicle* to the readers of *Newsline*—most of whom had probably never before heard of the newspaper. The implication was that the B.B.C. was under the influence of, or controlled by, zionists. *Newsline* also gave the irrelevant information that Young was a director of British Caledonian Airways. It is difficult to draw from this any other conclusion than that not only is the media zionist controlled but that zionism itself, a movement of the Jewish masses, was in fact created by Jewish capitalists. The National Front has also emphasised that the B.B.C. is chaired by a **"leading zionist"** *(Nationalism Today,* number 17). Fortunately for the credibility of communism this outburst from the W.R.P. was condemned by at least one other organisation as coming straight out of the Protocols of Zion *(Socialist Organiser,* 18.11.82).

The Socialist Workers Party has also articulated its own variant of the conspiracy theory—making the fantastic allegation about zionism that:

> **"It's essence is that a 'chosen people', the Jews, are superior to everyone else and should trample on the rights of other peoples". (20.10.73).**

This is incredible. A Marxist approach to the 'essence' of zionism would look at its social roots—which manifestly lay in the reaction of the Jewish masses to the pogroms of the late nineteenth and early twentieth centuries, and to Nazism. It seems that *Socialist Worker* imagines that zionism emanates from a mysterious plot in which Jews see themselves as the "chosen people" —a biblical reference which is seemingly equivalent to modern 'master race' theories and in which Jews believe themselves 'superior to everyone else'. The S.W.P. has substituted, at least on this occasion, a materialist analysis of zionism for an idealistic one—and one that is completely anti-semitic.

The logic of these politics within the S.W.P. was shown several years later (31.5.80) when it printed a letter from a certain Anthony Jones. Its ostensible purpose was to argue that the T.V. film "Death of a Princess" (which portrayed some of the more reactionary aspects of life in Saudi Arabia) somehow gave support to zionism. In reality the letter was grossly anti-semitic and was full of innuendos about Jewish control of the media. To quote:

"**Such is zionist influence in Britain—particularly in the media ('Lord' Lew Grade, 'Lord' Bernstein) —that this film was bound to be shown and therefore used to stir up anti-arab feeling".**

Anthony Jones was, in fact, one of the organisers of the National Front in Tameside. Even if the S.W.P. did not know this then the nature of the letter should have alerted them. However, *Socialist Worker* was seen to be quite unable to distinguish anti-zionism from blatant anti-semitism.

The attempt to invoke biblical images of the 'chosen people' to explain zionism as the latest example of Jewish power-seeking, is in fact found in diverse political sources. The unifying theme is that the Judaic religion is viewed as both the basis of zionism and as a faith which preaches genocide and the enslavement of gentiles.

*Spearhead* (December 1982) claimed that zionism was based on the belief by Jews that they were **"God's chosen people"**. The Stalinist soviet academic Kichko has written in his book *Judaism and Zionism* that:

"**Judaism teaches that Jews should force the subjugated people in the invaded lands to work for them as a people of priests".**

The Stalinist Vladimir Begun similarly wrote in his *Creeping Counter Revolution* that:

"**Zionist gangsterism… has its ideological roots in the scrolls of the Torah and the precepts of the Talmud".**

('Anti-zionism in the USSR' in *The Left Against Zion*, ed.

Wistrich, in which both the above books are quoted).

Even a revolutionary socialist magazine on the Middle East claims that the politics of zionism come from the Talmud. (Israel Shahak, 'The Jewish Religion and its Attitude to Non-Jews', *Khamsin*, issue 8, 1983). Actually, this particular article has a certain uniqueness amongst Left conspiracy theories, in that its author makes the claim, remarkable in a revolutionary socialist journal that:

"**An examination of radical, socialist and communist parties can provide many examples of disguised Jewish chauvinists and racists who joined these parties merely for reasons of 'Jewish interest' and are, in this region, in favour of 'anti-gentile' legislation".**

In other words, just as the Right claim that Jews enter communist groups in order to subvert capitalism so now a member of the Left claims that they enter such groups in order to subvert communism!

In 1982, *Labour Herald* (produced by several people prominent on the left of the Labour Party) published a book review and a letter by H.C. Mullin (March 19th and May 28th respectively). In his letter, Mullin said:

**"I assert that the Zionists use the lie that the Western democratic forces made no attempt to rescue Europe's Jews from the Nazi terror to instil guilt in the members of Western society. The reason being, of course, that guilty persons are easily manipulated in the services of zionism".**

In accomplishing this manipulation Zionists are allegedly able to control **"the right wing propaganda organs"** —in other words, the media. This really is 'revisionist' history of a major order.

Far from being a lie that the "democratic" forces made no attempt to rescue Europe's Jews, it is a patently obvious fact. Indeed for six years after the Nazis came to power, the Allies remained silent, attempting a policy of appeasement and an alliance with Nazism against the Soviet Union. At the same time, all the major imperialist countries imposed rigid immigration controls against Jewish refugees which continued to exist throughout the war, both in this country and in the U.S.A. For instance in 1942, the Vichy regime in France agreed to hand over 19,000 Jews to the Germans for slave labour and then extermination in Poland. Appeals were made to the British Foreign Office to take these Jews into the U.K., to which one official replied:

**"We cannot turn our country into a sponge for Europe".**

Those Jews who did manage to get here before the war were put into internment camps as 'enemy aliens'. Many were deported to Canada or Australia—a ship-load of deported Jews was sunk when the Arandora Star was torpedoed in July 1940. For many years even the existence of the concentration camps was denied or minimised on the grounds that (quoting another Foreign Office official):

**"As a general rule, the Jews are inclined to magnify their persecution".**

Throughout the war Jewish organisations made repeated requests to the Allies to bomb the gas chambers and incinerators at Auschwitz. They were told that such pin-point bombing was impossible. However, in September 1944 the U.S. airforce was able to bomb the I.G. Farben industrial complex which was immediately adjacent to Auschwitz. All these facts are well known to the survivors and have

45

been documented in such books as *Britain and the Jews of Europe* by Bernard Wasserstein (from which the above quotations have been taken).

Mullin's writings mirror the attempt by Nazi 'revisionist' historians to deny the murder of six million Jews. This is part of a similar attempt to portray Jews as manipulators of historical truth. As has been said in previous chapters, the Left has accused Zionists of exploiting **"the natural hatred of the labour movement for anti-semitism"**. It is also a Nazi ploy, as seen in a fascist magazine *Holocaust News,* to accuse Jews of 'exploiting' and exaggerating the holocaust. The opening line of its first editorial stated:

**"The Zionists used the 'Holocaust' myth to create a smokescreen of international public sympathy".**

As a socialist paper, *Labour Herald's* printing of Mullin's letter without comment, must be seen as complicity in the perpetration of anti-semitic myths. Furthermore, the real lie peddled by the Western bourgeoisie—namely that the last war was somehow a war against fascism and anti-semitism—remains unchallenged. The reality was that it was a war between two rival imperialisms, British and German—a rivalry that was perceived as too great to permit a joint alliance against the U.S.S.R. The fascistic and anti-semitic nature of the Nazi regime was absolutely irrelevent to Britain and the U.S.A., as neither declared war until their imperialist interests were threatened.

## Equating Zionism With Imperialism: Anti-Zionism Without Zion

The Left, or a section of it, obviously considers zionism a pretty powerful force. It controls the media. It finances British diplomacy. It rewrites history—and it also runs British Caledonian Airways. This is not merely reminiscent of the world conspiracy theory—it also has an uncanny resemblance to the hyperbole of that theory. It sounds very similar to Arnold White's belief, already seen, that Jews have done everything from 'baffling the Pharoahs to undermining the Third French Republic'.

In fact, the Left's conspiracy views are not just anti-semitic, they are also explicitly anti-Marxist. Thus zionism is not seen as merely furthering the interests of imperialism in the Middle East—which nowadays it undoubtedly does. Rather it is seen as in some way being the **same** as imperialism with the same international power. In other words the Left has not only an anti-semitic analysis of zionism but, in

46

common with all other adherents of the conspiracy theory, it has an anti-semitic analysis of the world. Indeed at times, zionism is portrayed as a form of world domination that is on an even higher level than imperialism itself, and is actually pictured as **controlling** imperialism. Thus *Newsline* (9.4.83) speaks of a zionist power **"stretching through Downing Street channels right into the White House"**. *Newsline* has obviously discovered a new law of the world's development. Lenin was presumably wrong when he analysed imperialism as being the highest form of capitalism: zionism is apparently even higher, as it is able to control the two main nerve centres of imperialism! This method of analysis has more in common with Stalinism than with revolutionary socialism. For instance *Pravda* (4.10.67) claimed that the United States—the most powerful state ever known to history—was itself a **"Zionist colony"** (quoted in Wistrich). This is truly looking at reality upside down.

This form of 'anti-zionism' transcends anything done by the Israeli state—or even the very existence of that state. It could just as easily exist without Israel, without zion and even without zionism. A 'socialism' which perceives zionist influence throughout the world, from Downing Street to the White House, stopping off at the B.B.C., is no different from the classic anti-semitic imagery of Jews being 'rootless cosmopolitans', without a state of their own, feeling no loyalty to any particular state but only to themselves. This imagery was much in vogue before the creation of the state of Israel. Stalinists still use it today—as in the Polish government's condemnation of K.O.R.* The imagery is the same, the existence of Israel is quite irrelevant. Anti-zionism without Zion has the same transcendental qualities as anti-semitism without Jews; it has no necessary relationship to anything a real zionist, or real Jew is doing. It exists in the air quite apart from material reality—except for the reality it creates for itself. Thus *Newsline* is full of imagery about 'links' and 'channels' and 'connections' that zionism is making between Caledonian Airways, the White House, the B.B.C. and the Jewish Chronicle. It also manages to make another 'zionist connection'—with the Manpower Services Commission whose chairperson happens to be the brother of the omnipotent Stuart Young. In exactly the same way, Arnold White in his book *The Modern Jew* talks of a Jewish **"subterranean and invisible influence"** and of the existence of a **"complex and mysterious power denied to any other living race"**.

* KOR—intellectual group influential with Solidarity in Poland

# The Collective Guilt Of All Jews For Zionism

The elevation of zionism to the equivalent of world imperialism and beyond is just one half of the conspiracy theory. The other half is the reduction of all Jews and all Jewish history to the zionist experience. There is a systematic tendency on the Left to define Jewish identity simply in terms of zionism. The natural corollary of this is to hold all Jews, wherever in the world, responsible for zionism, irrespective of what they actually believe. This is the theory of collective responsibility. In addition to all the examples given above, here are others which relate directly to the perceptions of collective guilt:—

A bizarre example, important not in its own right but for what it indicates, was the conversion in 1979 of Bob Dylan from the Jewish religion to Christianity. *Socialist Challenge* (the paper of the then International Marxist Group, now renamed the Socialist League) did not respond to this by any Marxist critique of the Christian religion or the Christian church. Rather it denounced Dylan as a zionist. In fact it denounced him as a millionaire zionist (27.9.79). This incidentally was just over a year after the paper had been raffling Dylan concert tickets!

Far more serious was the response by the Left to the Parish synagogue bombing on the Rue Copernic in October 1980. This was an openly fascist attack and was condemned by the entire Left, but this condemnation was equivocal. Most of the commentary actually concentrated on the **"opportunity"** the bombing presented to zionism! *Socialist Challenge* proclaimed that:

> **"The Israeli government is doing its best to exploit the bombing" (October 9th).**

Its editor Geoff Sheridan, in a letter to the paper, stated that:

> **"The Israeli government is quite cynical about the benefits it hopes to accrue from the fascist attacks in the diaspora" (November 27th).**

It is incredible that the significance which 'socialist' organisations accord to fascist attacks on Jews is mainly in relation to the reaction on the Israeli government. The Left in this instance reduced the experience of even dead Jews, murdered by anti-semites, as being nothing more than tools of zionist propaganda. Is the main criticism of Nazi Germany and the Holocaust now to be that it provided the "opportunity" for zionism? In fact, the National Front takes this to its logical conclusion by claiming that **"everybody in France knows"** that the Rue Copernic Shul was actually bombed by **"zionist terrorists"**—just as it claims the Holocaust was itself a zionist invention (*National Front News*, November 1982).

Equally significant was the Left's response to the machine gun and grenade attack on the synagogue in Vienna in August 1981, resulting in yet more deaths. Unlike the Paris bombing this met with virtual silence. There only can be one explanation for this: responsibility for the attack was claimed by a Palestinian splinter group. So it seems that all Jews are seen as legitimate targets because all Jews are somehow responsible for zionism. It is interesting to note that when this was raised with two of the larger Left papers they both denied such motives and claimed they did not have the 'space' to report such attacks (*Socialist Challenge*, 17.9.81; *Socialist Worker*, 26.9.81). The excuse of 'we haven't the space' has almost been developed into a scientific theory by the Left whenever outrages are committed against Jews. In the case of the Vienna attack, it would be farcical, if it were not tragic, and it is dishonest given the coverage of the openly fascist bombing a year previously.

## The Lebanon Invasion and the theory of Jewish collective responsibility

The Israeli invasion of Lebanon in 1982 was quite obviously an action that all socialists should have energetically condemned. However, it brought to the surface the ways in which the Left ascribes collective guilt to all Jews—for zionism in general and the Israeli government in particular. This was perhaps seen most clearly in the newspaper *Big Flame*—precisely because it was prepared to respond openly to criticisms made of its editorial policy.

*Big Flame* in its editorial of October 1982 stated that the massacres at Sabra and Chatilla **"cannot fail to spark off acts of revenge throughout the world"**. By "acts of revenge" is meant, presumably, the bombings and other attacks on Jewish institutions and individuals that occurred throughout the diaspora, following the invasion. What is remarkable is that *Big Flame* seems to think that these are 'natural' or 'inevitable'. The paper seems to consider that Jews who were bombed in, for example, Sydney Australia were legitimate targets—as if by being Jewish they were somehow responsible for what was happening in the Lebanon. It would be interesting to know why *Big Flame* doesn't think that acts of revenge were inevitable against Christians—given that the Phalangists were at least as responsible as the Israeli government for the massacre. It does explain, however, the complete silence of *Big Flame* in response to the actual attacks made on diaspora Jewry—they were never mentioned.

Once Jews everywhere are assigned a particular responsibility for what happened in the Lebanon, then other horrific assumptions follow. In particular, it is assumed both that Jews are under a greater moral obligation than anyone else to speak out against the invasion, and also that we have to speak out against it explicitly 'as Jews'. Why should we be obliged to speak out 'as Jews' about what is happening in the Middle East any more, for example, than Italians should speak out 'as Italians'? To be accepted as 'good' Jews apparently, the onus is on us to make public disavowals of zionism. Occasionally another hypocrisy creeps in; Jews 'of all people' should know better because of the history of our own oppression (*Big Flame* editorial, Sept. 1982). This is the ultimate double-standard. Jews are now expected to be on a higher level of morality than anyone else because of the oppression inflicted on us; but if we act immorally, or if any one Jew misbehaves, then we also have to apologise more than anyone else and make public penance. In fact, the theory that our own suffering should have cleansed our souls owes more to the gospels than to Marxism. What our suffering points to is the need to combat anti-semitism. It is no advertisement for the purity of our morals.

The entire Left described the Lebanon invasion by invoking the language of the 'holocaust' and the 'final solution'. This use of language is itself anti-semitic. This is not because the invasion was not murderous. It was. It is not because the slaughter of the Palestinians has not reached the number of Jewish people massacred by the Nazis—numbers are irrelevant. There is no scale of injustice as far as murder is concerned. The reason why the use of language such as 'holocaust' and 'final solution', when applied to zionism, is anti-Jewish is because these words are no longer neutral or objective. They have a particular political significance. They refer to Jewish people. In fact they refer to all Jewish people—because it was the genocide of all Jewish people that was contemplated in the final solution.

It is because these words have this precise political significance, a significance well understood by Jews, that they reinforce the idea all Jewish people everywhere are responsible for the invasion and the massacres. Words used to describe the collective predicament of Jews now prescribe the collective guilt of Jews. The September *Big Flame*, in responding to criticism, said that in describing bloody events

**"One's language can all too easily become looser, using terms**

50

> that fall into the hands of the oppressor. With Israel this is
> particularly the case".

It is difficult to know whether this is meant as an apology. It doesn't
even begin to explain why the actions of the Israeli government
should "particularly" reduce the Left to anti-semitism. Should we
now expect a racist analysis the next time a government of black Africa
operates in an oppressive way?

It is seen later that the ultimate trap placed in front of Jews by the
Left is that Jews themselves are responsible for anti-semitism. The
anti-semites are correct—everything is our own fault! This is the
destination to which the theory of collective responsibility leads.
Sometimes it is expressed quite explicitly. *Big Flame* (October, 1982)
stated that:

> **"zionism is the monster that is doing most to fuel anti-semitism
> in the modern world".**

This stands reality on its head. The crime of Begin, Sharon and the rest
of the Israeli government was the attempted destruction of the Palestinians as a nation. This is why they are to be condemned—and not for
any consequences their actions may have had on diaspora Jewry
(namely **'revenge'** which *Big Flame* seems to see as rational). Neither
Begin nor any other Jew, zionist or otherwise, is responsible for
anti-semitism. This is solely the responsibility of anti-semites. *Big
Flame* did apologise for this statement in its following issue, but
attitudes such as this are not simply 'mistakes'. They are intrinsic to
the way sections of the Left hold the entire international Jewish
community responsible for the actions of one, or some, or many, Jews.

## Zionism's Dominant Position Within Jewry

The fact that within certain Jewish communities, partciularly those in
Europe and the U.S.A., zionism holds a hegemonic position, does not
render the notion of 'collective responsibility' for zionism any less
anti-semitic. This is not simply because, even within these communities, there are countless Jews who are not zionists. More important is the fact that the anti-semitism of the 'collective guilt of Jews'
is based on the bizarre premise that non-Jews cannot be zionists or
supporters of zionism. Indeed in a political sense, Jewish people are
the least significant, the least powerful, advocates of zionism, since
zionism is hegemonic throughout the body politic of all Western
imperialism. There is no major political party which does not provide
it with its backing.

51

The creation of Israel was naturally impossible without Jewish struggle within Palestine, irrespective of outside help (which if anywhere came from Eastern Europe). However, the continued existence of Israel is due neither to its own resources nor to the help of diaspora Jewry. It is due to the political, economic and military support of the U.S.A. and its allies. There is a supreme historical irony present here. For two millenia Jewish people have been held collectively accountable for the action of any one Jew. This is simply one consequence of the theory of the world Jewish conspiracy to which zionism was a political response. Yet it is the hegemonic position of zionism within some Jewish communities which is today being invoked in order to 'prove' the conspiracy theory and to hold all Jews collectively liable. A frequent example is the way in which the full spectrum of political opinion refers to the 'Jewish lobby' in the U.S.A. as somehow controlling the foreign policy of the most powerful country in the world.

## The Distortion Of The Jewish Predicament

The Left does not simply have a perception of zionism as part of a Jewish conspiracy. Rather it grossly minimises the anti-semitism which gave rise to zionism, and completely distorts the Jewish response to anti-semitism. In spite of all its pretensions to the contrary, the Left provides no socialist or revolutionary alternatives to zionism. In essence, it wrongly portrays European Jewish communities as entirely passive in the face of anti-semitism, which is seen as invincible and unavoidable. Instead of struggling against anti-semitism, the Jew allegedly attempts to escape it by colonising Palestine and oppressing the Palestinians. This is the scenario of the Jew as passive victim or homicidal maniac. It has as much to do with political reality as Dr. Jeckyl and Mr. Hyde has to do with the reality of schizophrenia. It substitutes impressionism for serious analysis. This sort of approach has a long historical pedigree throughout the Left. Here are some examples:

The classic Marxist critique of zionism was Karl Kautsky's *Are The Jews A Race?* It is interesting, in the light of later criticisms of zionism, that Kautsky hardly refers to the national rights of the Palestinians. In fact he only mentions them as being an obstacle to the zionist enterprise. His objection is wholly on the grounds that zionism is a retreat from, a passive refusal to fight, anti-semitism. Thus he wrote:

**"It is not in Palestine but in Eastern Europe that the destinies of**

the suffering and oppressed portion of Jewry are being fought out. Not for a few thousand Jews or at most a few hundred thousand but for a population of between eight and ten millions. Emigration abroad cannot help them no matter whither it may be turned. Their destiny is intimately connected with the revolution in their own country".

Similarly, *Big Flame* talks of the establishment of the Jewish state as being an **"accommodation with the oppressor"** (Sept. 82).

It is, of course, a principled and correct socialist position to try and struggle, as long as is practicable, against oppression wherever it is found—though it hardly seems correct to put moral blame on the victim for fleeing from it. This book is definitely in favour of Jews staying as long as possible in this country to create a socialist revolution and, hopefully, to defeat anti-semitism. However, most socialists have adopted a position whereby Jews are expected to struggle in impossible situations, to become martyrs, rather than go to Palestine/Israel. Kautsky wrote the above in 1921. By 1939 it had become ironic.

The 'logic' of the statement by *Big Flame* that the creation of Israel was an "accommodation with the oppressor" is that Jews in Europe should have stayed around before (and during?) the war or returned later to fight anti-semitism. The truth is that no-one put up a serious fight against anti-semitism until it was too late. Germany itself is a classic example—as neither the parties of Stalinism nor of social democracy put up any effective resistance to the Nazis, in spite of the desires of many of their members. In this situation what would *Big Flame* have expected German Jews to have done (given that every major country imposed restrictions on their entry) other than have tried to get into Palestine? What does *Big Flame* think of Isaac Deutscher, the renowned Marxist intellectual and life-long opponent of Stalinism, who wondered in 1954:

**"If instead of arguing against zionism in the 1920's and 1930's I had urged European Jews to go to Palestine, I might have helped some of the lives that were later extinguished in Hitler's gas chambers"** ('Israel's Spiritual Climate' in his collected essays *The Non-Jewish Jew*).

It is no wonder that many, maybe the majority of Jews, still see Israel as a place of 'last resort' even if they do not consider themselves as zionists.

The Left does not only consider that Jews should martyr themselves, in the face of fascism. It also assumes that zionists will, in any event, martyr themselves by abdicating from the fight against anti-semitism. Thus Kautsky described zionism as something **"which amounts practically to a desertion of the colours"**. In like manner, *Big Flame* argues that zionism **"means giving up the battle against anti-semitism"** (Sept. 1982). The assumption appears to be that Jews are self-ordained victims who will go meekly to their deaths without struggle—or else will lapse physically or metaphysically, into the 'escapism' of the false Jerusalem of Israel. The myth that six million went to their graves like sheep is still prevalent everywhere.

It is actually inconceivable that the Jews could have waged a successful resistance, given their total isolation in the night of the holocaust. It does however, require a profound ignorance to be unaware that much-anti-Nazi struggle, both before and during the war, was led by a combination of Bundists (Jewish socialists) and Left zionists. The Warsaw Ghetto uprising, the first major civil uprising of the war, is just one notable example. There were many others. It is also a complete distortion of the position of zionists in other periods to imply that they simply submitted to anti-semitism. It is the caricature of the Jew as a masochist with an insatiable death wish.

At a time when major sections of the Left in this country were advocating the Aliens Act many zionists actively opposed it, Poale Zion (the workers' zionist movement) for one. At one of their meet-ings in Whitechapel a resolution was passed:

> **"This mass meeting declares that Jews must continue to work for their economic and political freedom in the lands of their sojourn"** (*Jewish Chronicle*, 26.5.1905).

The main opposition to immigration control came from Jewish socialists who were anti-zionists. However, it is simply a lie to claim that zionists have a perspective of never resisting anti-semitism. Again, in the 1935 general election a policy statement was issued by the Central Committee of Poale Zion emphasising the need for the Labour Party to join with Poale Zion in the struggle against fascism and anti-semitism (see essay by Knowles in collection of pieces on *Racism* edited by Robert Miles).

Finally, *Big Flame* criticises zionists, particularly Theodor Herzl (one of the founders of political zionism) as regarding anti-semitism as timeless and 'inevitable'. Some zionists do certainly think in this way. The Left escapes its responsibility, however, avoiding the critical question of why anti-semitism **does** appear inevitable to so many Jews. An answer to this would require a more complete analysis of the persistence of anti-semitism throughout different historical epochs and social formations. This has not yet been done by the Left. All that is forthcoming is the repetition of vacuous rhetoric. When reassessing the East European Jewish community of his youth, Isaac Deutscher wrote:

"The anti-zionist urged the Jews to trust their gentile environment, to help the 'progressive forces' in that environment to come to the top and so hope that those forces would effectively defend the Jews against anti-semitism. 'Social revolution will give the Jews equality and freedom. They therefore have no need for a Zionist Messiah'—this was the stock argument of generations of Jewish Left wingers. The zionists on the other hand dwelt on the deep seated hatred of non-Jews and urged the Jews to trust their future to nobody except their own state. In this controversy zionism has scored a terrible victory, one which it could neither wish nor expect; six million Jews had to perish in Hitler's gas chambers in order that Israel should come to life" (Deutscher, 'Israel's Spiritual Climate', *The Non-Jewish Jew* p.91).

In other words, it is only realistic that the onus should be on us as socialists to prove that anti-semitism is neither inevitable nor invincible.

## The Alternative To Zionism

Zionism has seen the expropriation, colonisation and dispersion of the Palestinian people. This obviously has to be opposed. One such necessary form of opposition is solidarity with the Palestinian struggle. However, it is wilful blindness to imagine that this will, in any way, undermine the social roots of zionism, because zionism was an attempted liberation struggle by the Jewish people. It was an attempt by Jews to free themselves from the noose of anti-semitism, at a time when no other way was apparently possible. Deutscher has written that:

"for the remnants of European Jewry (is it only for them?) the Jewish state has become an historic necessity". (Deutscher *The Non Jewish Jew*)

For zionists to believe that such a state is no longer necessary, it is vital to attack that which necessitated it—namely anti-semitism. When confronted by the spectacle of an arsonist firing a person's home, it is not morally justifiable for a passive observer to blame that person for jumping—even if s/he lands on a complete stranger. Certainly the stranger may be justifiably aggrieved—and with equal certainty cannot be expected to take responsibility for a fire they did not create. However, if no other homes are to be burned then the arsonist must be stopped. Moreover, isolated householders cannot be expected to do this unaided. As long as passers-by remain observers then the sorry saga will continue. The analogy with the triangle of the anti-semite, the Jew and the Palestinian is obvious. The onus for resisting anti-semitism cannot be on Jews alone. Wherever there is anti-semitism the socialist and labour movements have to oppose it. Unfortunately these movements have, all too often, been either passive or complicit.

# The Left's Advice to Jews—Assimilate and Stop Being Jewish

## Assimilationism

Running parallel with, and sometimes overlapping, the Left's infection by anti-semitism as an ideology is a chauvinistic attitude towards Jewish culture. The content of Jewish culture is never actually discussed by the Left. Jews are viewed as one-dimensional people. We are defined in terms of any combination of four variables: from one point of view we are defined in terms of religion or zionism, an irreligious, anti-zionist Jew is simply deemed not to exist; from another point of view our existence is reduced to being either aggressors through zionism or, less frequently, victims through anti-semitism.

Genuine questions which should be of concern to socialists—such as the class content of Jewish culture, or the effects of imperialism on that culture, or whether it is possible to talk of a single Jewish culture, or what is positive, and why, about that culture—are hardly ever mentioned. Instead there is the assumption that Jews should forget their culture and assimilate. This chauvinistic and reactionary attitude is also one that has long been held by the Western European diaspora leadership, which believes that assimilation is the route to 'acceptance'. It also accords with the practice of imperialism of which the British is probably the best and most successful example. Thus British imperialism, following its Christian tradition, is an expert at engulfing, invalidating and then destroying all 'alien' forms. When confronted by a socialist tradition, which in practice advocates the same process, it is no wonder that progressive Jews find it hard to assert an identity that is both Jewish and socialist.

## Left Orthodoxy

Assimilationism has today reached the status of a tenet of faith on the

Left. Like most faiths this 'gospel' is simply assumed and is normally made explicit only when challenged, when it is then stated as dogma. Thus the editor of *Socialist Challenge*, Geoff Sheridan, made the stark statement in relation to Jews that **"assimilation is not a process socialists would wish to halt"** (13.11.80). This immediately begs the question—assimilation into what? The only culture that Jews can assimilate into in this country is a racist, sexist, capitalist and anti-semitic one. If the revolutionary Left exists to promote this then it need not bother—British imperialism is possessed of far greater resources and experience. Support for assimilation is support for British chauvinism. In reality, socialist practice in the U.K. is simply to ignore, and therefore be complicit in, the fact that this is a WASP* country. Christian culture is somehow assumed dead and is in any event believed to stop at the church door. It is considered unremarkable that the leading 'revolutionary' press should have seasonal Christmas editions whilst the festivals of non-Christian cultures are ignored or regarded as opiates. Indeed, it is a spurious and peculiarly Christian atheism which allows British socialists to welcome public holidays (holydays) within the Christian tradition, but tolerates a system where members of other religions are compelled to work or take unpaid leave during their own festivities.

Within the Left there is the rhetoric of 'support' for national and cultural minority rights. However, the idea that there may be anything positive within Jewish culture is simply dismissed. Socialist practice extends only as far as liberal patronage. Lenin is the most obvious example. His writings on these matters are collected in *Lenin on the Jewish Question* edited by Hyman Lumer and where all subsequent quotations can be found. Lenin wrote:

> **"It is the Marxist's bounded duty to stand for the most resolute and consistent democraticism on all aspects of the national question"** (*Critical Remarks on the National Question*).

However, he immediately followed this by stating, **"This task is largely a negative one"**. In other words, Lenin seemed to regard the substance of most minority cultures as being either reactionary or non-existent. For instance, in referring to the Jews of Russia and Galicia (half the Jews in the world), he said that **"Jewish national culture is the slogan of the rabbis and the bourgeoisie"** (*On the National Question*). For Lenin the only alternative to ghettoisation was assimilation. A proper socialist position on these matters would permit and encourage a struggle within minority cultures against

* WASP—White Anglo-Saxon Protestant

their own oppressive elements, whilst simultaneously waging a struggle against the chauvinism of the host culture. Lenin, however, established Left orthodoxy by his advocacy of assimilationism combined with patronising toleration of Jewish culture. Thus John Nolan in a letter to *Socialist Challenge* talks about the existece of sexual oppression within 'Judaism' and states that:

> **"This is not incompatible with our defence of oppressed groups—even if they hold views incompatible with our views of socalism"** (1.1.81).

There is no recognition of anything beneficial within Jewish life—which is merely reduced to a matter of religion. In particular, there is no acknowledgement that there may be elements within Jewish culture which are in opposition to oppressive attitudes. It is interesting to know why John Nolan wants to 'defend' Jews—as he believes everything we stand for is incompatible with his views of socialism. Actually all he is willing to defend (if anything) is, apparently, the physical existence of Jews—our identity he will let rot.

To be specific, socialist practice disparages virtually everything to do with Jewish culture. Karl Kautsky, the leading Marxist theoretician of his period, wrote in 1914 of Polish Jewry that:

> **"They have preserved to this day a peculiar language, the so-called Yiddish, a corrupt German—the only Jewish population in the world that has not assimilated the language of its environment"** (*Are the Jews a Race?*, all further quotations from Kautsky can be found in this book).

Such a statement revealed a profound ignorance of other Jewish communities who had preserved their own languages. Most prominent were the Ladino-speaking Jews of the Mediterranean, whose great centre until the 2nd World War was Salonika. Ladino is still in use today in areas of the Balkans.

Moreover, completely lacking from Kautsky's observation was the fact that for several hundred years prior to the holocaust, Yiddish was the autonomous and rich language of daily communication for virtually all of East European Jewry. It was a wonderful vehicle for the expression of Jewish imagination—through poetry, prose and drama. Fundamentally, Yiddish was not simply a language. It was the basis of a whole cultural life—Yiddishkeit. Kautsky reduces all such vital manifestations of communal life—a life split as in every community by class conflict—to German dialect.

Lenin—who likewise seemed to think that Jews lived only in

MANCHESTER

# INTERNATIONAL WORKINGMEN'S

## Educational Club.

No. 8 ........ Date ..Feb.... 18 89

Name... W. William Wess

Occupation ...Printer......

W. Wess .......Secretary.

...Goldman.....Treasurer.

*Membership card of William Wess for the International Workingmen's Educational Club (Manchester). Note the Club's rules in Yiddish.*

Europe—was even more pernicious. In *Critical Remarks on the National Question* he divided Jewry into two groups—those from the East of Europe who were 'rabbis' and those from the 'civilized world' of Western Europe where:

> **"The great world-progressive features of Jewish culture stand clearly revealed, its internationalism, its identification with the advanced movements of the epoch".**

This is glib and patronising. Not only was the Marxist movement in Eastern Europe itself heavily composed of many Jews, not only is it left unexplained how 'rabbis' migrating West suddenly became proletarian internationalists, but Lenin displays complete ignorance in defining progressive elements within a culture exclusively in terms of its overt political expression. There is more to European Jewish culture than socialist thought—though this was certainly one of its achievements.

## Assimilation As An Answer to Anti-Semitism?

Throughout most socialist literature about Jews there is a judgemental attitude which suggests that Jewish people should assimilate in order to avoid anti-semitism. For instance, Lenin quoted Kautsky with approval, in relation to Russian Jews:

> **"Hostility towards non-native sections of the population can only be eliminated when the non-native sections cease to be alien and blend with the general mass of the population. This is the only possible solution to the Jewish question"** (*The Position of the Bund in the Party*).

The modern Left crudely repeats this. Nigel Ward in an article in *Socialist Challenge* gave as one explanation for the holocaust the fact that Jews in Western Europe were not **"assimilated into the fabric of Western society"** (2.10.82). *Big Flame* took this one step further when it claimed that Jews were attacked as they were **"visibly different"** (September 1982).

This advice that Jews should assimilate in order to avoid 'progroms' is startlingly reactionary for various reasons, some of which are examined later. For the time being, it is merely necessary to point out that the Left echoes the Jewish establishment, which also advocates assimilation as a way of avoiding political struggles against anti-semitism. Indeed, the Left is articulating a position which is almost identical to the 'aspects' of zionism that it attacks with the most vehemence. Thus zionism is seen as an avoidance of the necessity to

61

fight against anti-semitism—but this is precisely what assimilation-ism is. Furthermore zionism is criticised for presupposing an 'eternal anti-semite' who cannot be confronted but must be by-passed through the creation of some form of national ghetto. In a sense, Lenin's position is even more extreme. He seems to believe in the eternal anti-semite whom Jews can neither confront nor avoid but can only satisfy by **un**becoming Jewish.

## Jewish Survival Through Anti-Semitism?

The Left has a completely contradictory position on the relationship between Jewish survival and assimilation. It argues that assimilation is necessary for some form of survival, and simultaneously argues that Jewish culture and identity have only survived because of anti-semitism. Whereas all other groups exist in spite of, and in opposition to, their oppression, Jews exist as a result of it! Amongst the classic Marxist writers, the clearest exponent of this view was Kautsky who wrote that

> **"Judaism draws its strength—as a specific group segregated from its environment—from anti-semitism alone. In the absence of the latter it would have been absorbed long ago... When the Jews shall have ceased to be persecuted and outlawed the Jews themselves will cease to exist".**

Similarly Geoff Sheridan wrote in his letter to *Socialist Challenge*

> **"Jewish identity has been undermined in those societies where anti-semitism has become relatively dormant".**

Two examples will suffice to show that this view is not only politically suspect, but also obviously historically incorrect. In both Moorish Spain and immediate post-revolutionary Russia, Jewish culture flourished in relatively favourable circumstances. It is an anti-semitic myth that Jewish people have a 'victim mentality', but too much reading of certain 'Marxists' might make such a mentality appear necessary for the survival of Jewish identity.

## Determinism and Fatalism

Behind Left orthodoxy there is a crude historical determinism which is not only chauvinistic but also quite defeatist. This is the deter-minism which claims not only that assimilation is necessary to avoid anti-semitism, but that it is in any case historically inevitable. It was with specific reference to Jews that Lenin talked about:

> **"Capitalism's world historical tendency to... assimilate**

nations... which is one of the greatest driving forces transform-
ing capitalism into socialism" (*Critical Remarks on the National
Question*).

In similar vein, a Stalinist soviet scholar, Iosef Braginsky, has written
that:

> **"The Marxist cannot view assimilation from the narrow stand-
> point of 'dos pintele yid'. One has to realise that assimilation is a
> natural historical process"** (quoted by Lumer in his introduction
> to Lenin's writings).

The political consequences of this are predictable—namely a complete
fatalism and defeatism in the face of the projected disappearance of
Jewish culture. What is the point of struggling for something which
some pre-determined historical law has deemed to be doomed? In
fact, Otto Bauer, the Austrian Marxist active at the turn of the century,
stated this explicitly when he wrote:

> **"Where a whole nation are doomed to extinction by economic
> development it is petty-bourgeois, reactionary, utopian to
> oppose this inevitable course of events."**
>
> (quoted in Robert Wistrich—*Socialism and the Jews*).

A central feature of Lenin's writings is his hopelessness and
defeatism about the survival, let alone development, of Jewish
culture. As a renowned revolutionary activist, he nevertheless ex-
hibited a passive acceptance of the status quo as he saw it—namely the
disappearance of Jewish culture. It is scarcely believable that he was,
in the last resort, prepared to allow 'market forces' to determine
cultural progress. This was most evident in his attitude towards the
survival of Yiddish as a language. In '*Critical Remarks on the National
Question*' he argued, correctly, that revolutionaries in pre-revolu-
tionary Russia should be exposing the privileged status of the Russian
language as chauvinistic, since it was the language of all official state
documents and transactions. He suggested that Russia should have
several official languages on the model of Switzerland. Beyond that,
he was prepared to leave everything to capitalist anarchy. He wrote
that:

> **"The requirements of economic exchange will themselves
> decide which language of the given contry is to the advantage of
> the majority to know in the interests of commercial relations.
> This decision will be the firmer because it is adopted voluntarily
> by a population of various nationalities and its adoption will be
> the more rapid and extensive the more consistent the democracy**

**and as a consequence of it the more rapid the development of capitalism".**

This shows a touching faith in capitalist 'democracy' and its economic system. Completely lacking from this schema is any notion of struggle to preserve, popularise and validate a minority culture amongst the majority. There is no recognition of the fact that, for example, the disappearance of Yiddish within a generation in this country (capitalist 'democracy' par excellence) was not to be the result of any 'natural process', but was, rather, a political victory for cultural imperialism.

Finally, Lenin does not even consider the political option of members of a cultural and economic majority taking the initiative and learning about the cultures of other people—not as an academic exercise but in order to enrich themselves and communicate with others. In the absence of this, the struggle against anti-black racism by white people and against anti-semitism by gentiles, can never be more than a liberal and patronising platitude. The only sort of assimilation that socialists should be campaigning for is the assimilation of the majority into the minority, and not the other way around.

## Are the Jews a People—Class?

The most articulate expression of this determinism is to be found in Abram Leon's book—*The Jewish Question*. Leon was a Jew and a Trotskyist who perished in Auschwitz at the age of twenty six. His book is a major attempt at a Marxist study of the history of world Jewry and, incidentally, of anti-semitism. It purports to provide a materialist explanation to both the existence and the 'inevitable' disappearance of Jewry. Its central thesis is, however, untenable. Leon addressed himself to the question of **"the miracle of the Jew,"** that is the question why Jewry had survived so long in spite of persecution and martyrdom. His answer was that Jews had survived because of their economic role as traders and usurers and will disappear with the disappearance of those functions. As he said:

> **"Above all, Jews constitute historically a social group with a specific economic function. They are a class, or more precisely a people—class".**

There are many basic flaws in Leon's argument which have been pointed out by Maxine Rodinson in his preface to the French edition and by David Reuben (*Socialist Register*, 1982). Firstly, it is extremely

Euro-centric. As Reuben points out, Leon fails to consider Jewish communities where trade was not a significant feature, such as Jewry

**"...in the Byzantine Empire, the Yemen, the Falashim of Ethiopia, the Jewish farming communities of Daghesten and Kurdistan, the Jews in Babylon under Persian rule who were an agriculturally based community and the Jews of Cochin in India".**

Even assuming that Leon was correct, at least with respect to Europe, and that he could prove his assertion that **"the overwhelming majority of Jews in the diaspora engaged in trade"**, this would still leave unexplained the social situation of Jews which confined them to mercantile enterprise.

Moreover, Leon was historically incorrect even about Europe. European Jewry throughout its history seems to have been involved in occupations shared by the surrounding populations. For instance (at least at the start of the Middle Ages) land ownership was widespread amongst Jews in Western Europe. A further argument against the people-class theory is that even if some Jews were traders or usurers it is fantastic to reduce the survival of Jewry, as an identifiable grouping, to the role of a miniscule minority amongst them. Finally, Reuben emphasises that the idea of the survival of a people-class owing to its economic function only makes sense if that function was unique to it, and to no other group. In no sense, however, was either trade or usury a particularly Jewish preserve. The Church's opposition to usury was never strong enough to control it effectively amongst Christians, who were far more important economically than Jews. James Parkes has written (*The Jew in the Medieval Community*) that:

**"Compared with the effectiveness and ubiquity of Italian credit that of the Jews appears a very small affair and the part which they played in the Middle Ages has been much exaggerated".**

**"Throughout the period the chief moneylenders were Christian and apart from short periods and particular localities the Jews never played more than a subordinate role".**

In fact the **only** historical period—and this is debatable—when some Jews performed any unique economic function was that of inter-national traders between 700-1100 A.D. These merchants (Radanites) may have had a particular advantage, being neither Christian nor Muslim, during a period in which the Moorish control of the Mediterranean cut off normal trade routes between Western Europe and Asia. It was also in this period that there developed the vast Jewish empire of the Khazar Kingdom, stretching from the Volga delta to Kiev—the strategic importance of which was that it separated Christianity and Islam. In any event, the trading activities of the Radanites is hardly a persuasive explanation for the existence of world Jewry.

The excessive determinism of Leon's thesis can be appreciated when it is understood that it was an attempt to refine an even cruder version of the people-class found in Kautsky's *Are the Jews a Race?* Kautsky took the notion of 'survival of Jewry as a result of economic function' to its inevitable conclusion by arguing that Jews had become 'genetic' traders. He wrote:

> **"They must have developed emphatically those abilities needed by merchants and this great capacity must, in the course of many generations of such activities within the same families, have produced hereditary aptitudes and traits".**

So this is the view of a 'leading Marxist': Jewish culture has survived because of Jewish genes!

The conclusion that Leon draws from his thesis is as deterministic as its premise. He views assimilation as inevitable, precisely because the transition from feudalism to capitalism caused the alleged people-class to lose their functional role. He argues that:

> **"Capitalism destroyed feudal society and with it the function of the Jewish people-class. History doomed the people-class to disappearance".**

According to Leon the only reason Jewry remains a distinct entity is because of anti-semitism (which was also Lenin's position). Leon sees anti-semitism as a pre-capitalist caricature of Jews as usurers, which has survived into capitalism, in spite of the fact that Jews are 'no longer' usurers. He states that:

> **"Historically the success of racism means that capitalism has managed to channelize the anti-capitalist consciousness of the masses into a form that antedates capitalism and which no longer exists except in a vestigal state; this vestige is nevertheless still sufficiently great to give a certain appearance of reality to the myth".**

What Leon is saying here is that the existence today of some Jewish financiers is sufficient to evoke folk-memories of a time when the world was overrun by Jewish loan merchants—a time which, in fact, has never existed. According to his analysis, capitalist society needs a 'diversion' from the class struggle and this is provided by anti-semitism which, as well as facilitating assimilation, also needs to 'resurrect' the Jews. This is seen in his telling phrase, **"The Jewish masses find themselves wedged between the anvil of decaying feudalism and the hammer of rotting capitalism"**.

Abram Leon, as a Jew and a Trotskyist, had an absolute feeling for anti-semitism. He paid the highest price in the struggle against it when most of Europe had given up that struggle. But the deterministic conclusions in his book are just as erroneous as the deterministic premise on which they are based. We shall see late that anti-semitism cannot be viewed merely as a 'diversion' from capitalist crisis—rather it is a **constant** in daily life. Nor can it be viewed in any way as emanating from Jewish behaviour, if only retrospectively, as Leon suggests. It emanates from anti-semites. It does no justice to the richness and diversity of Jewish culture to suggest that it has continued and developed only as a result of anti-semitism.

The fundamental difficulty with Leon's work is that the original question he sets out to answer—what is the reason for the 'miracle' of Jewish survival?—is a strange one. A similar interrogative is not normally asked about any other people or group. No-one usually asks why the English, who have state power, or the Irish, who live in an occupied state, or the Romany gypsies, who have no territorial state, have survived. These could well be important and interesting questions, but why is the question asked only of Jews? The fact is that is is usually only religious Jews who ask Leon's question, and they naturally arrive at a theological solution—namely it **was** a miracle. It was to avoid such a conclusion that Leon appears to have adopted an ultra-materialist and deterministic analysis.

However, a materialist understanding of the world does not need to deny the intrinsic value of particular cultures. A proper study of Jewish survival would examine those aspects of Jewish culture which act as a positive and sustaining force, the very diversity of such culture being one main element. Indeed the diaspora—which many Jews understandably view as a negative experience—was in this respect a powerful force for expansive development. Hopefully, such a study would show that Jewish culture (or rather its progressive aspects) far from being doomed, has a role to play in socialist reconstruction. Unfortunately, the final conclusion of Leon's thesis is that socialism will have no place for Jewry or its culture, since its two supposed pillars—its economic function and anti-semitism—will have disappeared.

## Marx—The Assimilated Jew

It is ironic that Marx, in particular, is frequently paraded as an example of the way Jews should assimilate. John Nolan in his letter to *Socialist Challenge* writes that:

> **"We will be happy to persuade people to 'assimilate' along the road that Marx and Trotsky took away from their Jewish traditions towards the socialist revolution".**

It is significant that John Nolan counterposes the 'Jewish tradition' and 'socialist revolution'. It is as though Jewish revolutionaries and Jewish revolutionary organisations spring out of nowhere. Moreover Marx himself is a most disreputable example of where assimilation leads. He is a classic case of the self-hating Jew who has internalised his own oppression—albeit at a generation removed as Marx's father actually converted to Christianity. This is not to make the reactionary claim that Marxism as a philosophy is anti-semitic, rather it is to show that as an individual he had assimilated anti-semitism—the clearest example of which comes from his essay *On the Jewish Question*. This includes the following observations:

> **"What is the secular cult of the Jew? Haggling".**
> **"What is his secular god? Money".**
> **"Exchange is the true god of the Jew".**
> **"The chimerical nationality of the Jew is the nationality of the merchant".**
> **"The emancipation of the Jew is, in the last analysis, the emancipation of mankind from Judaism".**

Various apologies have been given for this diatribe. One is that the essay in question was actually written **in favour** of Jewish emancipation. However, as such, it was based on the worst form of liberal tolerance, as Marx obviously hated everything Jewish. Secondly, it is argued that Marx was not referring to any actual Jewish community but, in common with the language of his time, used 'Judaism' in an abstract sense to equate it with capitalist exchange values. For instance Nathan Weinstock has written that:

> **"Marx uses Judaism as an abstract category and does not seem to refer to any actual Jewish communities"** (see Appendix to *Zionism the False Messiah*).

However, even if Marx was using the term abstractly, then his language would be no less anti-semitic. Besides, Marx equated Jews and capitalism in very concrete, not abstract, imagery. Thus in the same essay he says of a Jew **"When he travels it is as if he carried his shop and his office on his back and spoke of nothing but interest and profit"**. Quite contrary to Nathan Weinstock, Isaac Deutscher tries to justify this article on the grounds that Marx, far from writing abstractly, was simply making **"a factual statement about the Jews' particular function in Christian society"** (see 'Who is a Jew?' in the collected essays *The Non-Jewish Jew*).

Apart from *On the Jewish Question*, Marx made countless other anti-semitic remarks in his writings. In his *Theses on Feuerbach*, he says that the German philosopher did not grasp the significance of revolutionary activity because practice is conceived by him **"Only in its dirty-Jewish manifestations"**. Furthermore, in a personal letter to Engels, he gave a description of Ferdinand Lassalle, a contemporary socialist, which managed to combine both anti-semitism and anti-black racism. He wrote:

> **"I see clearly that he is descended, as the shape of his head and hair indicate, from the negroes who were joined to the Jews at the time of the exodus from Egypt (unless it was his mother or paternal grandmother who mated with a negro). But his mixture of Judaism and Germanism with a negro substance as a base was bound to yield a most curious product. The importunity of the man is also negroid"**.

(Quoted by Silberner in an article on Marx in *Historia Judaica* 1949).

Paradoxically, Lassalle himself fits into the category of the assimilated Jewish socialist who eventually renounced everything in the Jewish heritage.

In what must be one of the most extraordinary love letters in human history he wrote to Sophie Sonstev:

> **"I do not like the Jews at all. I even detest them in general... During the past centuries of slavery these men acquired the characteristics of slaves and this is why I am unfavourably disposed towards them"**.

Elsewhere he wrote that **"There are two classes of men I cannot bear, men of letters and Jews—and unfortunately I belong to both"** (Silberner's article on Lassalle in the 1952-53 *Hebrew Union College Annual*). The epithet 'self-hating Jew' is an unpleasant one, but it is difficult to avoid its use in the case of both Marx and Lassalle. Neither are great advertisements for a liberated identity.

# Jewish Self-Organisation

Left assimilationism takes an organisational form in the frequent attacks on the notion of independent Jewish self-organisation. Whereas Kautsky's main reason for writing about Jews was to attack zionism, Lenin was mainly concerned with attacking the autonomous existence of the Bund—the revolutionary union of Jewish workers in Russia and Poland. Both used almost identical arguments. In fact, it is extraordinary that while Kautsky's criticism of zionism was in part based on a perception of the need for Jews to fight oppression, in whatever country they were living, when Jews did organise through the Bund to fight such oppression they were denounced as separatists. The Bund was an anti-zionist organisation, but their advocacy of autonomous Jewish socialist organisation led Lenin to denounce them for zionism (see *The Position of the Bund in the Party*).

Lenin launched a vast polemic against the Bund, superficially on the question of whether there was a 'Jewish culture' or a Jewish 'nation' —both of which he denied. Some of his positions were quite obscurantist: he went to exceptional lengths to 'prove' the Jews were not a 'nation'. In the *Position of the Bund* he quoted Kautsky's statement with approval: **"The Jews have ceased to be a nation, for a nation without a territory is unthinkable"**. This is sheer scholasticism. The ultimate logic of such an argument is that all diaspora Jews suddenly became a nation when Israel was established. In fact the whole debate is a complete abstraction. The political questions—for or against zionism of for or against self-organisation—cannot be 'solved' through a semantic debate about whether Jews have achieved the status of something which, like 'race' is completely metaphysical— namely 'nationhood'. To the extent that Bundists as well as Leninists—and as well as zionists—dealt in these abstractions they were all dealing in myths.

Nevertheless, behind all this obscuranticism, Lenin was attacking the very idea of the autonomy of Jewish political organisation. Some of his writings are very similar to criticisms made by sections of the Left today of independent black and women's organisations. This is perhaps most evident in his article *'Does the Jewish Proletariat Need an Independent Political Party?'* He attacked separatism on the grounds that:

> **"we must not weaken the force of our offensive by breaking up into numerous political parties, we must not introduce estrangement and isolation."**

This is precisely what is argued today against autonomous organisations, that they somehow weaken class struggle by initiating
divisions. There is a reluctance to acknowledge that class struggle is
already fragmented through, for example, sexism, racism—and anti-
semitism. Independent organisations of the oppressed are a way of
combatting this. In fact, Lenin specifically objected to the Bund for
daring to suggest that anti-semitism was not only found amongst the
bourgeoisie, but **"had struck roots in the mass of the workers."**
Finally, Lenin attacked the Bund for apparently referring to the
Bolsheviks as a **"Christian working-class organisation"** —just as
some modern Left groups object to being designated the 'white Left'
or the 'male Left'. What determines the categorisation of a political
organisation is not simple its aspirations, or its sociological membership, but also its attitude towards present oppression—and in this
sense it was understandable that the Bolsheviks should have been
considered 'Christian' by many Jewish revolutionaries.

## Assimilation and The Jewish Establishment

Lenin wrote that **"the best Jews have never clamoured against assimilation"** *(Critical Remarks)*. For Lenin, Jewry consisted of only two
groups—the 'rabbis' who advocated a cultural ghettoisation, and the
'progressives' who urged assimilation. He saw no third way. He
seemed ignorant of the fact that, particularly in Western Europe, it
was actually the anti-Communist Jewish leadership which was trying
to force the masses into assimilation. A correspondent to the *Jewish
Chronicle* wrote:

> **"To anglicise the Russian immigrant is a paramount duty... his
> children are in excellent hands at the Jews Free School but it is
> hard for the teachers of that institution to have to find their
> efforts partly neutralised by the fearful patois which their chil-
> dren have to hear, and often speak, at home... what is needed is
> some systematic apparatus for teaching English to adults and
> indeed for teaching them everything that is needed to make
> Englishmen of them"**. (31.7.1891).

The drive towards assimilationism, from within the community, was
a product of two interlinked motives which determine all actions of an
elite within an oppressed community. Firstly, assimilationism was an
exercise in class power by the establishment. It was an attempt to tame
the Jewish masses and as such the establishment were acting as pawns
for the British bourgeoisie. Indeed, the elite had highly personal

motives for this as some of them owned factories—particularly in the garment making industry—where their own Jewish employees had achieved high levels of militancy and socialist consciousness. A classic illustration of this was the attitude of the elite towards the development of a radical Jewish political forum. The *Jewish Chronicle* spoke disparagingly of the opening of an autonomous Jewish Socialist Club in Manchester where:

> **"A number of men and children were interspersed with a few women. A lecturer standing on a slightly raised platform held forth in "Yiddish" on the wrongs of the proletariat".** (3.7.1891).

This was one of several such clubs that sprung up in Manchester, Leeds and London. The response of the communal establishment was to sponsor alternative venues for Jewish workers where collaboration, not conflict, was the theme. The *Manchester City News* (7.2.1891) reported the opening of a Jewish Working Mens Club where the mayor and **"leading Jewish families"** were seated on a platform flanked by a banner with a portrait of the Queen and the motto **"God bless England, the land of freedom"**. In describing the club's activities the President noted that **"the only subject excluded was politics"**.

There was an additional motivation, as well as naked class interest, which led the elite to advocate assimilation. This was a direct consequence of anti-semitism. The fear this engendered lent the elite a self-perceived altruism—they saw themselves as responsible for the protection of the entire community. Protection, they believed, would come through assimilation. Assimilation did not mean a haphazard merger into the host community, but a conscious merging to avoid persecution. This consciousness has been a constant feature of the world view of the Western European Jewish establishment.

As early as 1888 the *Jewish Chronicle* was arguing that:

> **"If poor Jews will persist in appropriating whole streets to themselves in the same district, if they will persevere in the seemingly harmless practice of congregating in a body at prominent points in a great public thoroughfare, like White-chapel or the Commercial Road, drawing to their peculiarities of dress, of language, of manner, the attention which they might otherwise escape, can there by any wonder that the vulgar prejudices of which they are the objects should be kept alive and strengthened?"** (28.8. 1888).

Perhaps the most extreme example of the drive towards assimilation

# *Whitechapel &*
## *St. George's Branch.*

### *of the*

# *Socialist League.*

*................William Wess.................*

### *is a member of this Branch.*

*..........John Turner..........Secretary*

*..........May 1st.....1889*

*Socialist League membership card, 1889, for William Wess, a printer and prominent Jewish trades unionist. (see illus. 2 and 3)* can be found in the pocket book *'Helpful Information and Guidance for every Refugee'* issued in 1938 by the **"German Jewish Aid Committee in conjunction with the Jewish Board of Deputies"**. This was given to the few Jewish refugees who managed to pass through U.K. immigration control. It spoke of **"the traditional tolerance and sympathy of Britain towards the Jews"**, and then immediately went on to provide the refugees with a list of **"duties to which you are honour bound"** in order to avoid intolerance, including:

> **"Spend your time immediately in learning the English language and its correct pronunciation"**.
>
> **"Do not talk in a loud voice"**.
>
> **"Do not criticise any government regulation or the way things are done over here"**.
>
> **"Do not make yourself conspicuous by your manner or dress"**.
>
> **"Do not join any political organisation or take part in any political activities"**.
>
> **"Do not spread the poison of 'Its bound to come to this country'. The British Jew greatly objects to the planting of this craven thought"**.

The above attitudes only just stop short of advocating forced conversion for Jews! The impression gained from such material is that the elite had to stop short at some point if only to retain its own power base. In essence, they were calling for the abolition of the public expression of Jewish identity. From this perspective an analogy with the Marranos of Spain and Portugal, who though baptized, remained secret Jews, is not inappropriate.

It may well be that this combination of class interest and perceived altruism is what has historically defined the position of the Jewish establishment. Thus it also explains its support for immigration control at the turn of the century, which was seen as a way of both controlling and protecting those Jews already in this country. In any event, such a combination is absolutely prejudicial to the interests of the Jewish masses in that its whole thrust is to attempt to remove them, as far as possible, from progressive political struggle. In this country the Jewish bourgeoisie attempted to depoliticise the struggle against the Aliens Act, and then the struggle against fascism in the 1930s. An example of this is the attitude of the *Jewish Chronicle* towards the fascist march through Cable Street. Under the heading **"Urgent Warning"** the paper said:

> **"It is understood that a large Blackshirt demonstration will be**

**held in East London on Sunday afternoon... Jews are urgently
warned to keep away from the route of the Blackshirt march and
from their meetings. Jews who, however innocently, become
involved in any possible disorders will be actively helping
anti-semitism and Jew-baiting. Unless you want to help the
Jew-baiters keep away".** (2.10.36).

The attitude of the Board of Deputies, as expressed by its President
Nathan Laski at a public meeting in Shoreditch, was to rely on the
police and the Home Office (*Jewish Chronicle* 18.9.36). In answer some
Jewish militants replied in a letter aptly headed **"Did Judas Macca-
beus\* Stay at Home?"**(*Jewish Chronicle* 23.10.36).

All historical experience has shown that assimilation is never an
answer to anti-semitism. It can actually provoke further anti-
semitism. The habit of Jewish immigrants of anglicising their East
European names was, at the turn of the century, frequently pointed to
as an example of how Jews wanted to remain powerful but 'hidden'.
Even conversion is no defence—the Inquisition in Spain was
launched precisely to persecute the Marranos. Moreover, the drive
towards assimilation by the Western European and USA elite in the
last hundred years has itself had a disastrous historical consequence:
the Jewish masses are left confused about their Jewish identity, apart
from whatever relationship they have with zionism. One reaction has
been for sections of the Jewish youth of the last decade to hark back to
the past. There has been a mini-revival both of interest in Yiddish and
in Hasidic religious movements. However, all this is essentially reci-
divist and based exclusively on either nostalgia or obscuranticism.
Especially within Hasidism, there is a rejection of progressive movement for social change.

Matters of culture and the struggle against organised fascism are
equally 'political'. It is a pernicious form of liberalism which relegates
culture to the domain of the 'personal'. The truth of the feminist axiom
'the personal is political' is no more vividly obvious than in a response
to anti-semitism which calls for the abolition of Jewish cultural identity. One of the most startling realisations in reading the historical and
modern documents is how closely the assimilationism of the Jewish
elite resembles that of Lenin. Both expressly saw assimilation as an
'answer' to anti-semitism. Both were, and are, wrong.

---

\* Judah the Maccabee led the Jewish revolt against Syrian occupation in about 160 B.C.E.
He exploited ambush, night movement and rapid attack, in what was essentially a
guerilla campaign.

# Chauvinism or Anti-Semitism?

Assimilationism is undoubtedly reactionary. A generous interpretation of its acceptance by the Left is simply that it is an inadequate resolution of the 'national question' under socialism. Being less generous, however, assimilationism is a classic case of national chauvinism. It is based on the assumption that minority cultures have only a transient historical validity and inevitably have to disappear into the 'mainstream'. For example, Lenin saw only the Yiddish and not the Russian language as being an historical remnant.

Nevertheless, it is true to say there is a real problem in determining the relationship between the classic anti-semitism of the conspiracy theory and assimilationism directed by the 'host' community at Jews. Assimilation, unlike classic anti-semitism is not necessarily derived from Jewish conspiracy theories of history. It can be more frequently traced to the essential nationalism and chauvinism of the nation state. This is usually the case with the Left—which is capable of manifesting chauvinism to any minority, not just Jews. It would be ludicrous to see, for example, Bolshevik opposition to Bundist separatism as being motivated by conspiracy theories. The point is that the Bolsheviks were explicitly against separatism by any group! Indeed Lenin complained of the accusation of singling Jews out and said:

**"This is disseminating an outright falsehood for we have advocated denying representation not only to the Jews but also to the Armenians, the Georgians and so on".** (*The Position of the Bund in the Party*).

There is, nonetheless, a living relationship between national chauvinism against Jews and anti-semitism as an ideology. This exists on various levels. In the most general, but profound, sense both are firmly rooted in Christian perceptions. This is as true of the conspiracy theory as it is of the development of what was a European (and therefore Christian) phenomenon—the growth of the nation state. Significantly, Isaac Deutscher spoke not of European civilisation but of 'Christian-European civilisation' ('Who is a Jew' in *The Non-Jewish Jew*). Indeed, dependent on its period of social, economic and ideological development, the state was able to advocate either ghettoisation or assimilation as a way of 'dealing with' its Jewish population.

Even on the Left there is a ruthlessness and explicitness about advocating Jewish assimilation that takes it beyond the 'normal' bounds of chauvinism. The vocabulary used to describe the daily life of Jews—'doomed', 'extinct'—reads like a post mortem. In fact, it is correct to say that the policy of Jewish assimilation becomes part of anti-semitism; ideology precisely at the point where conspiracy theories are used to justify it. A classic case is the forced conversions of Marranos in Spain and Portugal as part of the relentless battle against Jewish devil-power. Nothing like this has occurred within Left anti-semitism, except perhaps the closing down of Soviet synagogues which is a step in this direction.

However, even in non-Stalinist sources, the conspiracy theory does sometimes raise its head in advocating assimilation. Occasionally this takes the form of crude anti-semitic imagery and analogy. Lenin could relapse into evoking the image of usury. He correctly criticised the Bund when they adopted two different constitutions—a minimum and a maximum programme (essay 'Maximum Brazenness and Minimum Logic'). However, he expressed himself as follows to the Bund:—

**"This is the positive last price not 'last word'. Only is it really your last, gentlemen? Perhaps you've got a minimal minimum in another pocket?... We very much fear that the Bundists do not quite realise all the 'beauty' of this maximum and minimum. Why, how else can you haggle than by asking an exhorbitant price, then knocking off 75 per cent and declaring 'That's my last price'? Why, is there any difference between haggling and politics?"**

He could hardly have been unaware of the anti-semitic stereotyping in this—echoing Marx's remarks **"What is the secular cult of the Jew? Haggling"**.

There is, though, a more consistent way in which anti-semitic theory is used to justify assimilationism. There is a repeated reference to the notion that Jews are pleading a 'special case' in trying to retain their own autonomy—either cultural or organisational. This is the 'uppity-Jew' syndrome. For black people the equivalent abuse means going above their status as slaves. For Jews it means trying to gain an ascendancy over others. We see in the next chapter that the idea that Jews are trying to gain special privileges is a recurring theme of the Left. In particular, it is alleged that Jews believe they are life's only victims. However, those Jews who oppose assimilationism are also branded as arguing a 'special case'. In *Socialist Challenge* John Nolan says, apropos of nothing, **"in the fight against oppression there are no special cases"**. Likewise, Lenin accused the Bund of 'exceptionalism' for advocating the maintenance and development of Yiddish and other aspects of cultural life. *(The Position of the Bund).*

Perhaps the clearest practical illustration of this accusation occurred in the Austrian Social Democratic Party. Its 1899 Brun conference contained a resolution suggesting that legislative power should be given to national minorities on a non-territorial basis. By this scheme, minorities were to be given power to legislate on their own cultural affairs, run their own schools and decide their own language. Irrespective of the merits of this attempt to resolve the national question—it was never passed—it is interesting that Jews were excluded despite the fact the Galicia was one of the world's largest centres for Jewry. Hence **"there are no special Jewish traits worth preserving. All retention of Jewish uniqueness is deleterious"** and:

> **"We cannot accept the separation of the Jewish proletariat in the realm of social life, which far exceeds the limits of ordinary national differences and finds its basis in religious and social conflicts"** (quoted in Wistrich-*Socialism and Jews*).

The idea that Jews who claim organisational and cultural autonomy are somehow claiming a special privilege, is a typical example of how Jews are put in a double-bind by the Left. Austrian social democracy shows that on the one hand the Left frequently does treat Jews differently from other groups, but on the other hand, when Jews dare point this out, they are accused of arguing a special case—that is they are accused of wanting different treatment! Indeed Lenin came close to asserting that in some ways the Bund's separatism was based on the belief that Jews were intrinsically superior to all other people—a classic anti-semitic jibe. He expressly accused the Bund of considering that **"The Jewish nation... occupies a special position amongst the nations"** *(The Position of the Bund).*

## Jewish Behaviour Seen as Responsible for Anti-Semitism

There is another relationship between the ideologies of anti-semitism and assimilationism. Assimilationism itself has various facets: it can refer to the categorisation of Jewish culture as inferior and even doomed; it can refer to condemnation of Jewish self-organisation. These attitudes are obviously also directed at other minority groups. However, Lenin has a particular argument that seems almost uniquely directed towards Jews—namely that we should assimilate as a political gesture in order to avoid persecution.

Lenin may have been sincere in his opposition to Jewish oppression, nonetheless his argument is, paradoxically, based on assumptions that are found in anti-semitism. If not anti-semitic itself it is still a capitulation to anti-semitism, as it locates the source of Jewish persecution not in the persecutor but within some perceived behaviour by Jewry—which Lenin himself described as **"non-native"** and **"alien"**. Such a description reads in terms very similar to those of the anti-semite Arnold White who attacked Jews for **"clinging to a community that prefers to remain aloof from the mainstream of modern life"** *(The Modern Jew)*. Of course it is central to the conspiracy theory that it is a response to some 'real' Jewish behaviour. The analogy with sexism is powerful. How would a 'socialist' analysis be received if it argued that to understand sexism it is necessary to examine, not the attitudes of men, but the behaviour of women? According to Lenin, Jewry must literally obliterate its identity not to be oppressed. In fact this sort of logic would have to tell women that the only way of dealing with sexism is to become men.

Unfortunately, a similar concession to the enemy occurs in the writings of Abram Leon. He treats anti-semitism as being a reaction to what he perceives as the Jewish historical role—namely trade and usury. Moreover, he views this as persisting even though Jews no longer perform such functions. In any event, he still locates the source of anti-semitism as being in some way linked to actual Jewish behaviour. Again, it is as though sexism were analysed as a reaction against the supposed behaviour of all women, or of some witches several centuries ago. Quite clearly, Leon's own personal and political practice—his revolutionary struggle to death against fascism and anti-semitism—was inevitably at odds with his theoretical model.

However, the crudity of such a model can be found in the statement made by Tony Greenstein, writing as chairperson of the Labour Committee on Palestine, that Nazism was built on **"the memory of the peasants regarding their relations with Jewish money lenders/tax collectors in feudal times"** (Letters Page *Big Flame* December 1982). This attributes an extraordinary memory to the German peasantry—it is as though there were no intervening anti-semitic ideology. It fails also to ask why the activities of Christian money lenders did not lead to the annihilation of most of Christendom several centuries later.

In fact, there has arisen a whole school of liberal historiography which acts as an apologia for anti-semitism precisely by arguing that it is somehow a reaction against real Jewish behaviour. A recent example is the book *Anti-Semitism in British Society* by Colin Holmes. Holmes explicitly acknowledges that he is engaged in an **"interactionist approach"** by which he means that **"in order to understand anti-semitic hostility we need to recognise the characteristics of the Jewish minority"**. In other words Holmes is saying that to understand anti-semitism we have to look at behaviour within Jewry.

The fundamental error of both revolutionaries such as Lenin, and liberals such as Holmes, is the belief that it is possible to discover a 'rational' source for anti-semitism. All such beliefs are premised on the assumption that there is some material conduct by Jews to which anti-semitism is a form of reaction, however perverse. Any genuine socialist understanding of anti-semitism requires not an examination of Jewish behaviour, but of the material behaviour of the anti-semite and of false consciousness. This is because, in spite of all its claims to the contrary, anti-semitism as an ideology has nothing to do with the behaviour of even one single Jew, let alone of all Jews. It is a view of the world based on myths and fantasies. To attempt to locate the source of such myths in Jewish life is ultimately a major concession to that ideology.

# The Politics of Terminology

It would, in the last resort, be dangerous to be rigid in reserving the terminology of 'anti-semitism' exclusively for a definition of the ideology of the Jewish conspiracy, and to use the language of 'chauvinism' to describe assimilationism by the host community. This is not just because the two may be **conceptually** linked, as has been seen. Rather they are also, as far as Jewish people are concerned, linked in daily life. To put it at its most basic, Jewish people feel trapped within their oppression. There often seems no way out. It is the totality of this oppression that is felt to be anti-semitic, irrespective of the theoretical origins of its components.

The historical periods detailed in this book are a good example of the mechanism of anti-semitism. Jewish people who, at the turn of the century, came to this country fleeing from pogroms, were met with conspiracy views on the Left. Such views have re-emerged today in the guise of anti-zionism, at a time when more and more Jews are beginning to find this racist country intolerable. Linking these two historical periods has been the constant propaganda of Left ideologues saying that Jewish culture is dead and urging Jews to assimilate, on the grounds that this is the only way to resist oppression. This succession of traps have in themselves gradually helped deter the Jewish masses from socialism as an answer to their problems. The most vivid illustration of this is that whereas zionism is attacked in part as avoiding the struggle against anti-semitism, Jewish self-organisation, such as the Bund, is attacked as being separatist and a concession to zionism!

These traps are just a faithful reflection of everyday reality as felt by Jewish people, where social life in gentile society is seen as one big double bind. There are many good Yiddish jokes about how we regard the slightest criticism as a form of anti-semitism, but these must be seen as a response to the way anti semitism often seems to be a closed circle, with no exit. It is not for the oppressor to deny the reality of the oppressed. It is not for Christian society to deny the potency of anti-semitism as an ideology, to deny the power of the theory of the world Jewish conspiracy. The historic effects of this theory have been dramatic. Not least it is the mechanism which starts and closes the circle of oppression around Jewish people: its inherent irrationality provides it with infinite elasticity.

Nothing can be understood about the Jewish predicament without understanding that what defines it as a unique category of racism is the existence of anti-semitism as ideology. It is this ideology that needs to be destroyed in order to give hope for Jewish liberation. This requires a serious political struggle—and one which is able to distinguish friend from foe. Assimilation is not the answer. It is part of the problem.

# Left Responses

When discussing Jewish people the Left has few remaining surprises. It is possible to guess the sorts of answers, often contradictory, that will be given to the critique of Left anti-semitism made in this pamphlet. One typical argument has already been seen—namely the absurd and insulting propostion that any discussion of anti-semitism is somehow an apolgia for zionism. There are, though, other replies that the Left makes with monotonous regularity. These are:-

## 'Jews Exaggerate Their Predicament'

Any attempt to uncover anti-semitism is branded as an **'obsession'** (*Big Flame* October 1982). This is part of the whole process of denying the significance of anti-semitism. Connected with this is the repeated accusation that Jews are arguing a 'special case'. We have already seen how this operates, in the sense that Jews are accused of wanting special privileges with respect to preservation of cultural and organisational autonomy, and that it is also used against Jews in the the sense that we are accused of considering ourselves the only victims in the world.

Such an attitude goes back at least to the early days of the Second International. For instance at the 1891 International Socialist Conference, the United States Jewish delegation, led by Abraham Cahan, wished the international labour movement to condemn anti-semitism—not an unreasonable request considering the pogroms taking place in Russia. Instead, the Congress adopted a resolution which opposed both anti-semitism and **"philo-semitic agitation"** (quoted in James Joll—*The Second International*). The phrase 'philo-semitic agitation' is highly significant and needs deciphering. At its best, it implies the identification of capitalism with a few Jewish capitalists—the essential socialism of fools. At its worst, it simply means 'Jew-lovers' —the essence of naked fascism. The 1891 conference must be unique in the history of international socialism, in that it is, presumably, the only instance in which friendliness towards any oppressed group was ever condemned by an international socialist body. *The Times* correctly opined that:

> **"The resolution in so far as it had any definite bearing on the Jewish question was deprived of any point it ever possessed"** (20.8.1891).

Even *Justice*, the paper of the SDF, admitted that

> **"There appears to be a strong feeling against the Jews in the Congress"** (22.8.1891).

However, in Justice's own opportunistic, and anti-semitic, tradition it added...

> **"This is a pity. Even on the grounds of tactics... we need the poor Jews to beat the rich Jews".**

Again in the last two thirds of this century it has been a frequent tactic to point out that it was **not only Jews** who were killed by the Nazis—the implication being that Jews consider they are the only victims of fascism. For example at a conference, organised in 1936 by the Labour Party against fascism, Hugh Dalton stated that there had been

> **"...excessive emphasis upon the fate of Jews in Germany—let us not forget the vast mass of gentile trade unionists, socialists and pacifists who have been subjected to atrocity and murder... Many millions of the best and purest Aryans have suffered",**

(quoted by Gisela Lebzelter in *Political Anti-Semitism in England*). Likewise Ed Rosen tells us that Gypsies also perished in the camps (*Peace News*, 21.3.80). Well, as Jews and as Socialists, we are well aware of the numbers and range of Nazi victims. All human life is of equal validity. However, it is also necessary to express the strongest possible disgust with those who deliberately invoke the sufferings of others in order to deny the extent of anti-semitism... including their own antisemitsm. It is a constant ploy of anti-semites first to victimise Jews and then to stigmatise Jews for 'wailing' and 'playing the victim'. Members of the Foreign Office, in refusing to help Jews trapped in Europe during World War Two, came out with such remarks as:

> **"One notable tendency in Jewish reports on this problem is to exaggerate the numbers of deportations and deaths"**
> (quoted in *Britain and the Jews of Europe* by Bernard Wasserstein).

So it is yet another double-bind for Jews: dare to cry out when you are being victimised and you will be accused of playing the victim, or else remain silent and be accused of being sheep led passively to slaughter.

## 'There Are Jews on the Left'

Many of the individuals criticised here and many members of the organisations criticised here are... Jewish. So *Big Flame* attempts to answer criticisms of its anti-semitism by asserting that its editorial board **"comprises both Jews and non-Jews"** (December 1982). However, this is tokenistic and naive if it is meant to 'prove' that *Big Flame* is not capable of anti-semitism. Obviously Jews, like everyone else, can internalise their own oppression. This, at one extreme, is what constitutes unconscious anti-semitism. At the other extreme, it is what constitutes the near-conscious self-hatred of Marx. None of this is to blame individual Jews in *Big Flame*. None of us could possibly claim to have a monopoly of wisdom in such hard circumstances and there are many routes to liberation. However, it is necessary to emphasise the very real existence of anti-semitism so that all of us as Jews have, at some level of consciousness, accepted certain anti-semitic attitudes as 'natural' and based on 'commonsense'.

## 'Criticism of Left Anti-Semitism Plays Into the Hands of Anti-Communists'

It will be claimed that this book is in some way echoing the views of the Jewish establishment, which seeks to discredit communism by asserting that the 'extreme Left' is exactly the same as the 'extreme Right' as both are anti-semitic. However such a claim is evasive, in that it does absolutely nothing to explain the substance and persistence of the examples of Left anti-semitism that we have quoted. It simply refuses to look at them.

Likewise, it may well be claimed that focusing on the anti-semitism of the Left only serves to draw attention away from the 'real' enemy—the fascist and Thatcherite Right. Again such a response is trivial, as it simply avoids acknowledging genuine ideological weaknesses on the Left. It is bizarre to expect that a socialist movement which so readily accepts anti-semitism could possible face up to the present offensive by the 'new Right', an offensive that will invoke anti-semitism more and more. Behind all this is an extremely dangerous assumption—namely that historical and contemporary truths should be suppressed in order to avoid further weakening the

Left. Such an approach has its roots in the Stalinist tradition of fabrication. The anti-communism of the Jewish establishment and the dangers from the British Right are perfectly obvious. This is why it is necessary to struggle against reactionary ideas both inside and outside the Jewish community.

At the same time, are those of us who are socialists and conscious of our Jewish identity supposed to make concessions to anti-semitism on the Left? Are we supposed to be grateful that the Left has not got a conscious policy of genocide? Is it supposed to make us feel any better that its anti-semitism often operates on a crass, unaware level? If Left anti-semitism is not as 'bad' as Right anti-semitism... then what perverse criterion should we be using as Jews and as socialists to convince ourselves of this? Would anyone seriously expect women and black people to stop challenging the Left whenever it operates on sexist and/or racist assumptions?

Moreover, the difference between 'Left' and 'Right' is genuinely problematic. It certainly cannot be taken for granted—no more in relation to Jews than with respect to any other matter of social or political life. It would seem absurd to describe Stalinism as 'Left-wing' even though historically it arose within the Bolshevik party. Similarly it is quite absurd to regard the distinction between Left and Right as self-explanatory in a situation where, for example, the National Front can claim the anti-semitism of the early socialist tradition as its own, and where *Socialist Worker* can print an anti-semitic letter from a known fascist. To define 'Left-wing' in some amorphous way as being 'the struggle against all oppression' is circular and apologetic, given the reality of the anti-semitism of so much Left practice.

Analysis of the Left/Right problematic in relation to anti-semitism does reveal two important differences. Firstly, anti-semitism is intrinsic to Right-wing ideology along with all other forms of reactionary ideas. The ultimate in Right-wing ideology, Nazism, can probably be reduced to anti-semitism. This is, of course, why it is so ironic that the Jewish establishment is constantly moving towards the Right. On the other hand anti-semitism is certainly not intrinsic to the concept of socialism or communism. Otherwise socialists would never struggle against anti-semitism whereas they actually do... on occasion. Indeed it would be grotesque to suggest, as members of the Jewish Board of Deputies never tire of suggesting, that the entire practice of the Left, on whatever issue, can be seen as expressions of anti-semitism.

The second distinction between anti-semitism on the Right and that on the Left exists on the level of consciousness. Anti-semitism operates on a more or less conscious level on the Right. Historically, there have been periods when anti-semitism has operated on a fairly conscious level on the Left—for instance in England at the time of the Aliens Act and under Stalinism. However, it is doubtful whether the Left could ever produce anything as conscious and as explicit as *The Protocols of Zion*. This would mean having expressly to abandon the theory of class struggle. In fact today the Left, at least outside Stalinism, seems to be functioning not so much on the basis of consciousness nor even of false-consciousness... but of unconsciousness.

Formally, the Left has a commitment to struggling against anti-Jewishness. The W.R.P., for instance, constantly proclaims its opposition to anti-semitism. Thus in its editorial in *Newsline* referring to 'The Money Programme', it stated in bold type:

**"The Tories know too that they have a powerful anti-semitic trump-card up their sleeve to replay once again as the most reactionary manifestation of racialism, which is anti-semitism"** (9.4.83).

At least this acknowledges the existence and obscene nature of anti-semitism, even though it still perceives it as a political tool rather than having an existence in everyday life. There is no reason to believe that the W.R.P., as an organisation, is not sincere in what it sees as its commitment to fight anti-semitism, and there is no reason to believe that any individual in the W.R.P. is a conscious anti-semite. Unfortunately the anti-semitism of the W.R.P. takes place on an apparently unconscious level. If the W.R.P. took time to consider, it would, hopefully, see that an editorial which claims that a B.B.C. programme was **'zionist sponsored'** and then goes on to remark that the new chairperson of the B.B.C. is a director of the *Jewish Chronicle* can only lead to one conclusion in its readers' minds, namely that the B.B.C. is itself zionist sponsored—i.e. controlled by zionists. Indeed in the absence of even a mention of the politics of the *Jewish Chronicle* (a journal whose politics no socialist would wish to defend but which, albeit occasionally, has printed articles critical of zionism), the obvious conclusion is that the B.B.C. is 'Jew sponsored'. Any group which claims to be against anti-semitism should be ultra-vigilant in the imagery it evokes—particularly when it also introduces irrelevant information about the financial interests of individual zionists. Actually, this lack of awareness is both ironic and frightening. The assumption is supposed to be that it is the Left and not the Right which operates on the level of consciousness—at least a consciousness of what it is saying. In relation to anti-semitism it often appears the other way around. Moreover, though it would help marginally, it is ultimately inadequate to argue that **all** the Left should do is to exercise greater 'editorial vigilance'. It first has to develop a consciousness of the anti-semitism against which it has to be vigilant—starting with its own. It is a tragedy that a movement based on the theory of consciousness has diverged so far from it in its own practice.

## 'Anti-Semitism Is A Series of "Mistakes" '

Many people will wish to face up to the existence of Left anti-semitism. However, they will be confronted by an argument based on a crude empiricism, which claims that instances of Left anti-semitism, though undoubtedly reactionary, are simply 'mistakes' or are 'merely' manifestations of false consciousness. In this scenario, socialist practice has generally been exemplary towards Jews, and on the question of anti-semitism, and all that has to be done is to lop away the reactionary ideas that 'occasionally' still crop up. After all—it will be claimed—even socialists are not perfect. This last claim, which is undoubtedly correct, is really based on the assumption that what is required is simply more 'vigilance'.

Now it is, fortunately, true that there does exist an alternative socialist tradition which has consciously refrained from anti-semitic positions or even opposed anti-semitism and which, in some instances, has even taken a positive attitude towards Jewish culture.

Engels in his famous *Anti-Duhring* attacked Duhring for, amongst other matters, his rabid Judeophobia—as witnessed by Duhring's statement that **"socialism is the only power which can oppose population conditions with a strong Jewish admixture"**. Similarly Lenin, in spite of his reactionary advocacy of Jewish assimilation, took a totally principled position against pogroms of any sort. For instance, in a decree of July 1918 signed by Lenin it was stated that

> **"The Council of People's Commissars instructs all Soviet Deputies to take uncompromising measures to tear the anti-semitic movement out by the roots. Pogromists and pogrom agitators are to be placed outside the law".**

(Quoted by Hyman Lumer—*Lenin on the Jewish Question*). Again the Trotskyists of the Socialist Workers Party in the U.S.A. campaigned in the late 1930s against the immigration quota imposed on Jewish

87

refugees from Europe by the U.S. government (*Socialist Appeal* 29.10.38)—though the Fourth International, to which it was affiliated, was in favour of total control of Jews going into Palestine. Trotsky himself seems to have developed an extremely enlightened attitude towards Jews—indeed an attitude which was extraordinary, when compared with that of other revolutionary Marxists. In an interview he gave in 1937 to a Jewish paper in Mexico, he effectively attacked crude assimilationism by stating that:

**"The Jews of different countries have created their press and developed the Yiddish language as an instrument adapted to modern culture. One must therefore reckon with the fact that the Jewish nation will maintain itself for an entire epoch to come".**

In an article—*Thermidor and Anti-Semitism*—published in 1941, he acknowledged that a revolution does not immediately or inevitably dissolve anti-semitism and that it can even provoke it as:

**"History has never yet seen an example where the reaction following the revolutionary upsurge was not accompanied by the most unbridled chauvinistic passions, anti-semitism amongst them".**

Interestingly, this led him, a confirmed anti-zionist, into envisaging the need for a Jewish state after a world revolution! (all quotations from Trotsky's writings *On The Jewish Question* by Pathfinder Press).

There has also been in this country at least one socialist organisation which took a principled position on everything Jewish—from opposing anti-semitism to refusing to define Jews negatively and only in terms of anti-semitism. This was the Socialist League in the last century. The League, as has been mentioned, through its activities and through its journal *Commonweal* consistently opposed the agitation for Jewish immigration control. At the same time, it explicitly denounced all anti-semitic imagery of Jews, opposed chauvinistic notions that Jewish workers were in competition with British workers, and preached unity and internationalism. The League regularly publicised, and actively involved itself in, the emergent Jewish labour movement in London, Leeds and Manchester. The League had particularly good relations with the important Jewish anarchist movement in London's East End—with whom Peter Kropotkin also identified and worked. On top of all this it is important to remember that countless socialists fought before and during the war, not simply against fascism but also wth a consciousness of a struggle against anti-semitism.

All the above instances are worth recording. However, the following has to be said to put them into perspective:—

Struggling against anti-semitism is the bare minimum requirement for a correct socialist practice in relation to Jewish people—but this is just the negative side. What is also necessary is a recognition of the positive aspects of Jewish culture, tradition, history and aspirations.

Moreover, even when the Left has organised against anti-semitism, this has often been in spite of itself and because of the pressures put on it by its Jewish members. Examples of this have already been seen in relation to the Aliens Act. Perhaps the most vivid illustration of the pressure of Jewish socialists on their own organisations concerns the 'battle of Cable Street' in October 1936, when the Mosleyites were physically prevented from marching through London's East End. The Communist Party has, in its own mythology, always taken credit for this as an almost single-handed operation. However, as Joe Jacobs, a Party activist at that time, shows in his autobiography, *Out of the Ghetto* , the Party at first argued against going to Cable Street. It was only pressure by its, mainly Jewish, Stepney Branch and by the militant Jewish People's Council which forced the Party to mobilise against the fascists, thus compelling them to make a complete volte-face two days before the march.

Finally, the citing of relatively favourable attitudes on the Left towards Jews only touches on one particular issue. This is the relative weight of the anti-semitic tradition within the Left. **It does not explain the existence of that tradition.** Instead, it assumes that Left anti-semitism can be viewed in some vulgar pragmatic way as a series of 'mistakes'. This is an expiricism which denies the persistence of anti-semitism on the Left and does nothing to explain its cause. It starts with the 'imperfection' of individual socialists who have been corrupted in some way by bourgeois ideology and ends up simply by calling for 'greater vigilance'. In fact, it does nothing at all to resolve the essential question of methodology. The obsessive insistence on highlighting examples of good socialist practice in relation to Jews, is an attempt to avoid bringing out into the daylight the distinct pattern which lies behind Left anti-semitism—namely the theory of the world Jewish conspiracy.

Of course, in an important sense, it is true that the existence of this pattern, this methodology, represents the penetration of the working class movement and its socialist ideologues, not only by bourgeois but also by feudal and pre-feudal ideology. It is a question of false consciousness. However, it is simply insufficient to state this without defining precisely what 'consciousness' it is that is false. This consciousness is the theory of world Jewish domination.

Avoiding looking at how the conspiracy theory has entered the Left means either denying the existence of Left anti-semitism, or viewing it as a series of unrelated and unexplained examples. It is absurd to regard the illustrations presented in this pamphlet—for instance the notion peddled by the SDF that 'Jew moneylenders now control every foreign office in Europe'—as being simply 'mistakes' by 'psychologically imperfect individuals'. Rather we are dealing here with the reactionary politics of mass psychology which does not just exist as an individual phenomenon. The Left also shares this mass psychology.

Inevitably this empirical approach to (mis)understanding Left anti-semitism is the exact mirror image of the empiricism with which bourgeois historians treat the whole of anti-semitism. According to much bourgeois historiography, anti-semitism is simply a string of 'false accusations'—Jews ritually kill Christian children, Jews poison wells, Jews desecrate the host, Jews are usurers, etc. etc. Such an analysis again totally avoids the question of how such 'false accusations' arose in the first place and how they fit within the context of the conspiracy theory. It does not attempt to locate the underlying ideology which unites them and which gave rise to their existence. Like all empirical philosophy, it is concerned with appearance—the use of particular anti-semitic imagery—rather than with essence.

Moreover by seeing anti-semitism as nothing more than a series of 'mistakes' which need to be 'corrected' by rational argument, this empiricism also reveals a compartmentalised and over-rational approach to consciousness. It believes that anti-semitism can be overcome by pin-pointing certain 'mistaken ideas'—e.g. Jews ritually kill Christian children—held by particular individuals and then by explaining the 'truth'—e.g. Jews **don't** ritually kill Christian children. Such transparent nonsense totally fails to understand the theory of a world conspiracy that underlies and sustains all anti-semitism, the history of this theory (which stretches back to the early days of the Christian church), and the mass psychology which gives it its political strength.

None of this can be overcome by a process of individual re-education, as it is not simply an individual problem. Nor can it be

*Manchester Jewish anti-fascists demonstrate in support of Republican Spain, circa 1937.*

overcome by a rational presentation of facts—as the last thing anti-semitism is about is rationality. This emphasis on individualism and rationalism is the hallmark of liberalism. Unfortunately it has a dangerous pedigree as far as an attempt to resist anti-semitism is concerned. In the 1930s, the Jewish Board of Deputies argued against confrontation with the fascists, and instead employed researchers to investigate and publicise the 'real' contribution that Jewish people had made to humanity. Indeed this is still the position of the Deputies today. Moreover, in the 1930s it was also the official stance of the Labour Party to invoke an appeal to 'facts' to refute fascist assertions about Jews (see essay by Caroline Knowles in *Racism* edited by Robert Miles). This belief that a liberal rationalism can somehow defeat a negative irrationalism, somewhat in the manner of the collapse of the walls of Jericho, avoids facing up to the need for a political struggle against anti-semitism. Such a struggle will inevitably have to take place on the level of emotionality as well as intellectuality. It will have to defeat the mass psychology of fascism and anti-semitism.

# How The Left Does Not Fight Anti-Semitism

## Left Modesty

There is one particular response from the Left, when presented with accusations of its own anti-semitism, that is almost liturgical in its repetition. This is the vanity which leads not merely to protestations that the socialist movement has actually opposed anti-semitism, but to the claim that it has consistently been in the vanguard of all such opposition. For instance, John Nolan (letters *Socialist Challenge* 1.1.81) made the modest claim that **"in the struggle against all forms of oppression, including anti-semitism, the I.M.G. and Socialist Challenge have proved themselves to be amongst the best of working class fighters"**. The Stalinists have made a similar claim about their own organisations. Hyman Lumer in his preface to *Lenin on the Jewish Question* states that the official Communist Parties **"have been the most resolute fighters against all national and racial discrimination and oppression"**. The sect may change, but the catechism remains the same!

Enough has already been presented to reveal the misplaced arrogance of this. How could a socialist practice which has internalised so much anti-semitism be in the forefront of resistance to it? However, it is relevant to go behond this and to criticise much Left practice even on those occasions when it is apparently opposing anti-semitism. The point is that this opposition often, at its best, severely underestimates anti-semitism and, at its worst, is complicit in it by accepting its terms. Either way, it ultimately rests on a refusal to see anti-semitism as an ideology.

## Complicity in Anti-Semitism

There have been periods in this country, as elsewhere, when sections of the Left, far from fighting anti-semitism have threatened to unleash pogroms against Jews. An article in *Justice* claimed that socialists

**"have no feelings against Jews as Jews, but as nefarious capitalists and poisoners of the wells of public information we denounce them. It would be easy enough to get up a capitalist Jew-bait here in London if we wished to do so"** (21.1.1893).

It is, incidentally, not insignificant that the medieval accusation of Jews poisoning the water wells reappears under a different guise in imperialist England. Moreover the S.D.F, like many other 'socialists' believed that pogroms were a prelude to an anti-capitalist revolution. Thus Hyndman applauded popular attacks on Jews in Austria on the grounds that:

**"The attack upon Jews is a convenient cover for a more direct attack upon the great landlords and Christian capitalists"**
(*The Historical Basis of Socialism*—1883).

However, the reality is that even where the Left has purported to struggle against anti-semitism it has frequently compromised itself with anti-Jewish feelings.

For instance the most classic form of compromise is to appeal to anti-semites to fight fascism! If Hyndman could call upon anti-semites to destroy capitalism (as represented by Jews), then it is equally 'logical' to call upon anti-semites to fight fascism as a manifestation of capitalism. In 1937 the Left Book Club published a book by G. Sacks entitled *The Jewish Question*. This proclaimed:

**"Hate the Jew if you must but do not allow your hatred to make you the victim of the fascist who, on the plea that he also hates the Jew, makes you his accomplice in worse crimes".**

Sacks then went on to point out that what was wrong with fascism was not its attacks on the Jews but that these attacks were no guarantee of a better society, thus:

**"If fascism really meant the end of the class struggle, then the humiliation and destruction of sixteen million Jews would be worthwhile, for the ultimate benefit to humanity would transcend that of a small minority of people who would scarcely be missed".**

In other words the 'explanation' we have previously examined, that anti-semitism is just a series of 'mistakes', appears here in its ultimate form—namely as a total concession to anti-semitic ideology.

It would be wrong to see this form of complicity as being confined to the Stalinist and social democratic tradition around the Left Book

Club. Thus the *Big Flame* editorial of September 1982 actually stated that as a socialist response to the Israeli invasion of the Lebanon **"it would be a serious error to participate in or help incite the emergence of a new wave of anti-semitism"**. The use of the word 'error' implies that the question of unleashing pogroms is merely one of tactics. The perverse logic of this is that if anti-semitism acted as a break on the Israeli government then it would in some way be legitimate.

Even amongst those on the contemporary Left fighting fascism, there is occasionally a residual belief that Jews are somehow legitimate targets for popular hatred. For instance Ed Rosen in an article in *Peace News* (21.3.80) wrote that the Nazis used anti-semitism in order **"to break the power of a privileged Jewish economic community"**. In other words, German Jews were supposedly rich and powerful—so what else could they expect? They asked for it. Indeed, we have already seen that advocating asimilation, as an answer to anti-semitism, itself rests on the assumption that there exists something actual and tangible in Jewish behaviour to which the anti-semite is merely responding.

## Denying The Significance Of The Material Consequences Of Anti-Semitism

Anti-semitism is essentially a view of the world, an ideology, yet of course it does have material and atrocious consequences for Jews—witness the 'final solution'. However the Left has systematically under-estimated these material consequences as can be seen in the following examples.

The holocaust is seen as unique and without any historical precedent. Thus Nigel Ward has stated that anti-semitism did not exist in Eastern Europe until the penetration of capital in the last century (*Socialist Challenge* 2.10.82). He ignores centuries of pogroms, often sanctioned by the Orthodox churches, not the least of which were the atrocities perpetrated by Chmielnicki in 1648, when an estimated one million Jews were killed—only those accepting baptism being spared. Chmielnicki is still regarded in the Ukraine as a national hero. Similarly, Ward claims that the economic position of Jews in Western Europe was **"threatened by the development of early capitalism"** after the eleventh century. Quite apart from the historical error of an assumed Jewish economic position—the word 'threatened' suggests some minor material decline. The reality was the constant attacks on Jewish communities throughout the Crusades. These in fact were repeated shortly afterwards, during the period of the Black Death (1348-9) when Jews were blamed in popular mythology for the plague. In Germany alone, over 200 communities were exterminated whilst attacks took place on a smaller scale in Poland, Catalonia and in the north of Italy.

The other side to the perverse view that the holocaust was without precedent, is the equally perverse notion that anti-semitism disappeared with the holocaust. *Big Flame* criticised those whom it claims **"hark back constantly to the history of anti-semitism"** (October 1982). In other words anti-semitism exists only in 'history'—though *Big Flame* does have the grace to admit that the 'tiniest elements' might still be around today. This is not simply reactionary. It is ahistorical and seems to be based on the liberal and social democratic myth that anti-semitism was defeated by the bourgeoisie in World War Two... as though this were somehow seen by the Allies as a war against anti-semitism. The same politics occurred in the propaganda slogan of the Anti-Nazi League in the middle of the 1970s—**"Yesterday it was the Jews, today it is the blacks"**. This imagined that somehow anti-black racism didn't exist at the time of pre-war fascism and that anti-semitism disappeared after, and as a result of, imperialist war.

There is another particularly insidious aspect to this constant under-estimation of anti-semitism. This is the appalling attitude by the Left that Jews will have to have one foot in the grave before it will respond. By this time, of course, it will be too late anyway. Thus Uri Davies (*Peace News* 26.1.79) was anxious to stress that

> **"Given the current social and political circumstances prevalent in Britain, anti-semitism does not feature as a prominent element in British racism... Jews in Britain are not the first nor the worst victims of racism. There is no denial that in future, given certain social and political developments, racism directed against Jews could figure more prominently in British society. But this is a contingent possibility and not a present development nor a likely development in the near future".**

It is not claimed that Jews are either the 'first' or the 'worst' victims of racism—and such was certainly not claimed in the article to which this was a reply. However, it is remarkable that any attempt to draw attention to the existence of anti-semitism can result in such slanderous assertions. The message appears to be that there is a queue or hierarchy of victims, and Jews will have to wait till they get to the front before anyone will take any serious political notice. Uri Davies seems to have a touching faith in the present social order. He should remember the misassessment of August Bebel who, in spite of his active opposition to anti-semitism, said in 1906 that **"It is comforting that in Germany it will never have a chance to assert a decisive influence on the life of state or society"** (quoted by Silberner in an article on German Social Democracy, *Historia Judaica* 1953).

Paradoxically, although the reality of Jewish oppression is often denied, the Left still persists in defining the Jew as a victim, but in a purely abstract way. However, this status is a surrogate one to play us off against different groups. A coarse example was the statement by Ken Livingstone, the Labour leader of the Greater London Council, that the suffering of the Irish at the hands of the English was worse that the Nazi holocaust of European Jewry. Who are statements like this supposed to help? Certainly not the Irish, who have an autonomous existence, and don't require their oppression to be validated by a league table with other groups. Neither do they help the Jewish people who are in any event being constantly told that their oppression is near the bottom of any league table.

Even when certain socialists claim that the Left has constantly fought anti-semitism, they have a totally restricted meaning of what anti-semitism is. They ignore and leave unopposed the anti-semitism of daily life on which fascism is ultimately built. For the Left, anti-semitism only seems to exist, if at all, when matters get to the stage of organised violence on a mass scale. There is absolutely no recognition of the profoundly anti-semitic culture which underlies these physical manifestations. It is as though major physical violence against Jews is an aberration which springs out of nowhere. There is a reverse side to all this. This is that anti-semitism without physical violence is deemed simply not to exist. Cultural imperialism is just ignored. As has been emphasised, the Left actively advocates assimilationism.

## Denying The Significance Of Anti-Semitism As An Ideology

Central to the socialist compromise with anti-semitism, and the underestimation of its material consequences, is the failure to perceive anti-semitism as an ideological force existing in daily life. It has already been emphasised in the previous chapter how anti-semitism is wrongly seen as a series of 'mistakes' made by its proponents. There is a reverse side, though, to this analysis. Anti-semitism is viewed as a series of tactical manoeuvres by the bourgeoisie designed to mislead the workers. The conventional wisdom of the Left is that 'pogroms' are simply a diversionary tactic by the ruling class: for tactical considerations the ruling class spreads false propaganda about Jews in order to induce erroneous perceptions in the rest of the workers. It is often presented as openly as this. For instance, the *Daily Worker*, then the paper of the Communist Party, stated that anti-semitism was a vehicle **"to divert the attack upon the capitalist class as a whole into an attack upon a section of that class—the Jewish section"** (2.3.1933). In similar vein and in the same period, A.M. Wall, the Secretary of the London Trades Council, in addressing a meeting called by the Jewish People's Council in London's East End, said

> **"Anti-semitism has always been used for the same purpose—in order to give the masses an enemy to attack so they won't discover the real enemy"** (*Jewish Chronicle* 16.10.36).

This analysis permeates every single part of the Left and can easily be found today. Thus *Big Flame* in its editorial of September 1982 explained anti-semitism by asserting that Jews are used as 'scapegoats' in periods of crisis. *Newsline*, as has already been seen, described anti-semitism as a 'trump-card' which the Tories have 'up their sleeves'. In other words, anti-semitism is viewed as some form of magic trick that is kept hidden until a period of capitalist crisis, and is then used to divide the workers—who apparently have not been previously divided by it.

This is a nonsense. People are already divided by reactionary ideas of all kinds. Anti-semitism exists in daily life. It does not need a conspiracy of the bourgeoisie to convince people. Anti-semitism may be, in Marxist terms, ruling class ideology, in that it arguably serves the interests of any particular governing class. However, it has also developed a relative and extremely strong autonomy over the last two millenia. It is genuinely believed by all clases.

One of the reasons why Nazism was so successfully expansionist right through Europe and into parts of the USSR, was because there was a large measure of popular support for the anti-semitism that was explicitly central to it. For instance, Polish Jewry was under increasing attack in the years prior to the Nazi take-over, and at least one village to which Jews returned after the Nazi defeat suffered massacres in 1945. The myth that Jews went like sheep to the slaughter is parallel to the myth that the mass of the local populace throughout Europe was either ignorant or immobilised through fear. The holocaust had popular support in many places in the occupied countries. Indeed, complicity in the 'final solution' is now a national scandal in France today.

However, just as people like G. Sacks tried to win anti-semites to the anti-fascist cause, so today some of the Left seek to deny the popular appeal of the Nazi anti-semitism. They do this by disputing the centrality of anti-semitism to Nazi theory. Thus Ed Rosen in his article in *Peace News* wrote that anti-semitism was a **"sideshow"** with Nazism. He also stated that **"both before and after Hitler came to power anti-semitism was never a mass movement in Germany"** and that it occurred only **"periodically"** under the Nazis. The assumption is that the Nazis did not believe their own anti-semitic ideology. It was just a tactic—and not an important one—that could be turned on and off like a tap. This is almost the 'reductio ad absurdam' of the denial of the mass appeal of the ideology of anti-semitism as an explanation of the world. To present this ideology as a tactical 'invention' by fascist demagogues to divide the workers, simply misunderstands the depths of its roots.

Moreover, behind this lies a completely cynical amoralism which exists today with respect to the struggle by Left groups against anti-black racism. The suggestion is that racism of any kind is not to be opposed for its own sake, but because it divides the class. Socialist ideologues are apparently immune to it by definition. Within the class, it is simply an 'error'. The logical conclusion of this is that Jewish people, along with everyone else, should not be fighting anti-semitism because it is anti-Jewish, but because it divides the class! Indeed, A.M. Wall actually did say that in the struggle against fascism... **"It was necessary for the Jews not to talk of themselves as Jews"** as this was somehow divisive. There is another logical conclusion to this: where there are no Jews, or where all Jews have been massacred and there is no longer a danger of class division, then presumably anti-semitism is permissible.

# The Non-Jewish Question

The few serious contributions by socialist writers towards understanding Jews and Jewish history are normally entitled 'The Jewish Question' (Abram Leon's book) or 'The Jewish Problem' (Isaac Deutcher's essay on 'The Russian Revolution and the Jewish Problem'). Also, reactionary writings on this subject have similar titles—for instance Marx's article and Sack's book on 'The Jewish Question'. What is really at issue here is a **non-Jewish problem.** It is a non-Jewish problem every time a Jew on the Left comes out as Jewish and is immediately requested—with grave suspicion by the person making the request—to give their position on... zionism. No questions are ever asked, either on a personal or a political level, about other aspects of Jewish identity or Jewish culture, or anything that might conceivably be positive about being Jewish. Every single contemporary quotation referred to in this book originates either in articles by the Left on zionism, or alternatively in articles by the Left responding to criticism of anti-semitism by Jewish socialists.

Non-Jews have an independent responsibility to face up to the power of anti-semitism in all its aspects—including anti-semitism within the Left. It should not always be up to Jews to take the initiative. The tragedy is that much of the socialist tradition, far from being a liberating force, is actually part of the problem.

It is unfortunately true that many of the criticisms made in this pamphlet can be made of the Left in all its activities—and not just in relation to Jews.

Generally speaking, the Left has a hierarchical view of oppression: it ignores questions of culture; it is threatened by separatist organisations; it has an ignorance of history in general and of its own history in particular. In a sense this book is merely a detailed examination of these matters through the specific illustration of how Jews are perceived. There are Jewish socialist organisations which are trying to (re)create an unoppressive socialist tradition in this country. As Jews we hope we have particular experiences that can enrich this. However, this book also has a very particular purpose. This is to try and make sense of the recurring examples of anti-semitism on the Left, and to show that they form a coherent pattern, based on the notion of the Jewish conspiracy. It is intolerable that the socialist movement has never been prepared to look at its anti-semitism in a self-critical way.

Moreover, there are four specific factors which stand out in this pattern and which illuminate it:
The first is the extraordinary popularism within the Left—in which it appeals to 'common sense' views that often make it genuinely indistinguishable from fascism. A lot of the writings quoted in this pamphlet, about Jews at the turn of the century, and about zionism, could have come directly from anti-semitic journals. The result is that papers like *Socialist Worker* actually print anti-Jewish letters by known fascists.

This book is primarily about Left anti-semitism in Britain. Nonetheless the examples drawn from this country are by no means unique. The tendency to rely upon popular anti-semitism can be seen as intruding into the whole tradition of European socialism. Robert Wistrich in his book *Socialism and the Jews* has recently shown its prevalence in the early social democratic parties in Austria and Germany at the turn of this century. These parties were mass organisations. Their extreme popularism can be seen most clearly by the fact that many of their leaders welcomed the victory of Karl Lueger's notoriously anti-semitic Christian Social party, in the 1895 Vienna municipal elections, as a prelude to the anti-capitalist revolution. Incidentally, an article by Derek Mahon in the *New Statesman* (which supports the Labour Party) has recently described Lueger as a "socialist" (9.9.83). At the same time, Jews who raised the question of anti-semitism were accused of pleading a 'special case'. For instance, in 1911 the myth of the blood libel reappeared in Russia when Menahem Beilis was accused of the ritual murder of a Christian boy. This led to violent anti-Jewish propaganda. Victor Adler, the leader of the Austrian socialists rejected requests to hold protest meetings in favour of Beilis and was reported as saying **"Jews and more Jews—as** if the whole world revolved around the Jewish question".

The 'Left' is obviously not a monolithic block. It has distinct strands and differing traditions. Left anti-semitism, though, has never been confined to any one particular socialist tradition—as well as being found within Marxism and the reformism of social democracy, it also appears within the anarchist movements. The following information is taken from E. Silberner's article on Bakunin in *Historia Judaica* 1952. Bakunin is regarded as a hero by most anarchists because of his theoretical writings and practical activities. In fact he was a complete anti-semite. He wrote that:

**"The whole Jewish world constitutes one exploiting sect, one people of leeches, one single devouring parasite closely and intimately bound together not only across national boundaries but also across all divergencies of political opinion".**

Bakunin also attacked Marx for being Jewish—just as Marx attacked Lassalle and Lassalle attacked himself!

Indeed, Bakunin's own justification of anarchy was remarkable in that it was founded explicitly on his own belief in the world Jewish conspiracy. He saw both capitalism and communism as being based on centralised state structures at all times controlled by Jews. He wrote

**"This Jewish world today stands in large part at the disposal of Marx on the one hand and of Rothschild on the other. This may seem strange. What common ground can there be between communism and the big bank? Oh! but the communism of Marx wants a powerful governmental centralisation and where this exists there must inevitably be a central State Bank and where such a bank exists the parasitic Jewish nation, which speculates in the labor of the people will always find means to exist".**

In addition to this the Narodnaia Volia (the People's Will Party) of Russia—a pre-Bolshevik organisation with strong Bakuninist and popularist tendencies—completely adapted to anti-semitism to the point of fermenting pogroms. Its executive committee issued on September 1st 1881 a proclamation urging the masses to revolt against the 'Jewish Tsar'.

**"Only blood"**, declared the proclamation, **"will wash away the people's affliction. You (Russian peasants) have already begun to rebel against the Jews. You are doing well. For soon over the whole Russian land there will arise a revolt against the Tsar, the lords and the Jews. It is good that you, too, will be with us".**

In conclusion, Jewish socialists who are today trapped within the innumerable double-binds of Left anti-semitism and who often doubt their own stability as voices crying in the dark should take heart.

Left anti-semitism is not a figment of anyone's imagination and it is not an 'obsession' to protest against it. There have always been Jews within the socialist movement who have protested and not let their pain remain secret or their anger unheard. Theodore Rothstein, then a member of the Social Democratic Federation, condemned that organisation's anti-semitism as an **"indelible burning stain"** on socialism (quoted by Ernest Bax in *Justice* 28.10.1899). Likewise, another member of the S.D.F., M. Shayer, wrote to *Justice* saying that the politics of that paper would ensure that **"Jews have no guarantee that they will enjoy peace and equality even in a socialist regime"** (7.10.1899). Though these protests have been long buried... we should revive them and swim against the tide in order to create a genuine socialism.

# Bibliographical Sources

Writing this book has been like both a voyage and a detective series. I have had to follow up references from many different sources. In doing so I have learned a lot. I am aware that one of the difficulties in discussing the matter of Left anti-semitism is a certain shared ignorance amongst socialists, Jewish or otherwise, of the historical material and where to locate it. In fact anyone who claims to be an 'expert' in this area is just a fool. It was to help encourage other people to read the material that I have encountered that I have included the references in the main body of the text.

However, some people have suggested that I compile a list of the main books (as opposed to periodicals or newspapers) that I had the pleasure (or lack of) to read. These were

J. Buckman, *Immigrants and the Class Struggle—The Jewish immigrant in Leeds*, Manchester University Press, 1983

E. Butler, *The International Jew*, Adelaide 1948

N. Cohn, *Warrant for Genocide*, Eyre and Spottiswoode, 1967

L. Dawidowicz, *The War Against the Jews 1933-45*, Pelican, 1979

I. Deutscher, *The Non-Jewish Jew*, Merlin Press, 1981

L. Gartner, *The Jewish Immigrant in England*, Simon Publications, 1973

C. Holmes, *Anti-Semitism in British Society 1876-1939*, Edward Arnold, 1979

J. Jacobs, *Out of the Ghetto*, Calverts North Star Press, 1978

K. Kautsky, *Are the Jews a Race?* Greenwood Press (Connecticut), 1972

G. Lebzelter, *Political Anti-Semitism in England 1918-1939*, Macmillan, 1978

A. Leon, *The Jewish Question*, Pathfinder Press, 1970

H. Lumer (ed.), *Lenin on the Jewish Question*, International Publishers (New York), 1974

K. Marx, *On the Jewish Question*—This is included in Early Writings on Marx, Penguin, 1975

R. Miles and A. Phizacklea (ed.), *Racism and Political Action in Britain*, Routledge and Kegan Paul, 1979

L. Trotsky, *On the Jewish Question* (a collection of writings), Pathfinder Press, 1970

B. Wasserstein, *Britain and the Jews of Europe*, Clarendon Press, 1979

N. Weinstock, *Zionism the False Messiah*, Ink Links, 1979

A. White, *The Modern Jew*, London, 1899

A. White (ed.), *The Destitute Alien in Great Britain*, London, 1892

W. Wilkins, *The Alien Invasion*, London, 1892

R. Wistrich, *Socialism and the Jews*, Associated University Press, 1982

R. Wistrich (ed.), *The Left Against Zion*, Vallentine Mitchell, 1979

# Shifra—Jewish Feminist Magazine

**Shifra** was a Jewish woman whose surname (sire-name) is unknown. Active in the Warsaw Ghetto resistance, she chronicled the suffering of her people. She was caught by the Nazis on the Aryan side of the city, tortured and murdered in 1943.

There have been many thousands of courageous Jewish women—we know very little about their lives and experiences. We choose **Shifra** because she speaks to us in her own name and not in the name of a father or husband. **Shifra** symbolises our purpose in creating this magazine.

**Shifra** is a collective of eleven Jewish Feminists—with at least twelve opinions—continuing the Jewish tradition. On the other hand, the Jewish tradition for the most part describes the experience of Jewish men. Our tradition is woman-centred. We want to claim our heritage as Jewish women.

We believe that since Jewish experience has been and is defined by Jewish men and women's experience has been defined by white gentile culture—even in the Women's Liberation Movement—it is essential for us to redefine the words 'Jewish' and 'Feminist' from our points of view. We recognise the mutual needs of Black and Jewish women (including Black Jewish women), and all women who experience racism, to organise autonomously around our oppressions.

As Jewish women:
- We are creating a feminist home in the Jewish community and a Jewish home in the feminist community.
- We see ourselves as firmly rooted in a diverse and fluid Jewish tradition;
- We are committed to fighting all forms of oppression;
- We celebrate our Jewish women's heritage;
- We affirm the presence of centuries of Jewish women.

**Shifra** is for, by and about Jewish women. We ask Jewish women to send contributions to **Shifra** which encompass our tradition in all its forms, including poems, stories, articles, pictures, biographies, songs, recipes, news—everything that concerns us as Jewish women.

**Shifra** will be a 48 page quarterly magazine, offering space to express the diverse experiences of Jewish women. We hope that **Shifra** will develop a broad circulation both in Britain and internationally—we have already made contact with sisters in Israel, Europe, America, Canada and are making efforts to contact Jewish women elsewhere.

Projected publication date: Chanukah 5745 (December) 1984.

**Shifra:** Box No 2, 59 Cookridge Street, Leeds LS2 3AW England.

**Shifra** collective: Bev Gold, Elizabeth Sarah, Francesca Klug, Jane Black, Leah Ruth, Libby Lawson, Linda Bellos, Marilyn Fetcher, Riva Krut, Scarlet Pollock, Sheila Saunders.